A
SILENCE
AND A
SHOUTING

Meditations and Prayers

by

Eddie Askew

© The Leprosy Mission International
50 Portland Place, London W1N 3DG
1982
Reprinted 1982
ISBN 0 902731 21 1

Printed and photoset by Stanley L. Hunt (Printers) Ltd. Rushden Northamptonshire

To Barbara, with love
and respect

English Parish Church

Foreword

THIS book of meditations began in a series of monthly
newsletters circulated to The Leprosy Mission's
workers worldwide. Suggestions of publication followed
and, in preparing them, the author has added prayers and
drawings to carry the reader's thoughts further.

Eddie Askew, with his wife Barbara, has served with The
Leprosy Mission for thirty-two years. First in India for
fifteen years, where their two daughters were born, and
more recently in the Mission's international office in
London. Since 1974, he has been International Director.

Introduction

BOOKS on prayer are published so often these days that to read them all would leave very little time left to pray; but I have been using one recently called *It's me, O Lord* by Michael Hollings and Etta Gullick.* There is a description of prayer which is more of a poem and a meditation than anything else. Here it is:

"The important thing about prayer is that it is almost indefinable. You see, it is: hard and sharp, soft and loving, deep and inexpressible, shallow and repetitious, a groaning and a sighing.

"A silence and a shouting, a burst of praise digging deep down into loneliness, into me. Loving. Abandonment to despair, a soaring to heights which can be only ecstasy, dull plodding in the greyness of mediocre being — laziness, boredom, resentment.

"Questing and questioning, calm reflection, meditation, cogitation. A surprise at sudden joy, a shaft of light, a laser beam. Irritation at not understanding, impatience, pain of mind and body hardly uttered or deeply anguished.

"Being together, the stirring of love shallow, then deeper, then deepest. A breathless involvement, a meeting, a longing, a loving, an inpouring."

Prayer is . . . resentment . . . irritation . . . impatience. Does that surprise you? It took me a long time to learn to bring my resentments to the Lord, as well as my joys and requests. Yet I think we should. Our whole lives should be, *are*, open to God and He knows what is there deep down. It is only by bringing our anger and irritations out into the open that He can deal with them, even direct them, for good. That is good psychology, and it is good Christian living too. And in the cleansing process comes the realisation and experience of love — shallow, then deeper, and a real meeting and involvement with the Lord.

*Published by Mayhew-McCrimmon, Southend-on-Sea

Lord, teach me to pray.

It sounds exciting, put like that.
It sounds **real**. An exploration.
A chance to do more than catalogue
and list the things I want,
to an eternal Father Christmas.

The chance of meeting you,
of drawing closer to the love that made me,
and keeps me, and knows me.
And, Lord, it's only just begun.
There is so much more of you,
of love, the limitless expanse of knowing you.
I could be frightened, Lord, in this wide country.
It could be lonely, but you are here, with me.

The chance of learning about myself,
of facing up to what I am.
Admitting my resentments,
bringing my anger to you, my disappointments, my frustration.
And finding that when I do,
when I stop struggling and shouting
and let go
you are still there.
Still loving.

Sometimes, Lord, often —
I don't know what to say to you.
But I still come, in quiet
for the comfort of two friends
sitting in silence.
And it's then, Lord, that I learn most from you.
When my mind slows down,
and my heart stops racing.
When I let go and wait in the quiet,
realizing that all the things I was going to ask for
you know already.
Then, Lord, without words,
in the stillness
you are there . . .
And I love you.

Lord, teach me to pray.

Psalm 139:1-12

THIRTY people, patients and staff, sat around the chapel in the leprosy hospital at Karigiri in South India. It is a lovely building in the local grey granite, designed in Indian tradition, flat roofed and open-sided to the air. The sanctuary is framed in carved wood, and behind the communion table soft light filters through a cross-shaped window in the stone and reflects gently from the polished floor. It is a Wednesday in Lent and the doctor — also an ordained minister in the Church of South India — was leading a service of meditation and prayer, one of a regular series of Wednesday evening services for Lent. He spoke quietly and reflectively, but with assurance and conviction. One phrase in particular struck me, and I've been thinking about it since. "There is no hiding place from God, but in God."

Many of the tensions which people experience today, whether they admit it or not, are caused by running away from God; running away from a commitment they are unwilling or frightened to make. In his perceptive and sensitive poem, *The Hound of Heaven*, Francis Thompson speaks from his own experience. He tells of his own running through the years, through the labyrinthine ways of his own mind, trying desperately to hide from what he thought of as a demanding and pursuing God. But like the Psalmist he found no escape: "Whither shall I go from thy spirit? or whither shall I flee from thy presence? . . ." (Psalm 139). At last, turning to face God he finds, not the frightening, devouring power he had fled from, but the open arms of welcoming dynamic love. The tensions are resolved, the alienation gone, sin is forgiven. The point of shelter from the strains which God's demands make, is in God Himself.

Much of the stress in our lives comes from our flight from the totality of commitment. We run from responsibilities we don't want to accept. We run from confrontation because we lack the courage to look at ourselves in the clear light of God's presence. We run because total commitment demands more change in our lives than we have the courage for. Yet running, we never arrive; we find no hiding place, nowhere is safe from God; and the only way to come to terms with the tension of God's presence is acceptance. We turn to face Him and we find, as Thompson found, that God's arms are the arms of healing love, arms "strong to heal and save". The point of resolution of the stress of God's demands is acceptance. The hiding place from God is in God; the point where life begins is at the Cross, in the death of self where "I no longer live but Christ in me."

Lord, you ask so much.
There was a time when I offered you everything.
In the rosy glow of commitment
nothing was too much, nothing too good for you.
I thought that once the decision was made,
once I put myself in your hands
then I could float, buoyed up, soothed, comforted
in the warmth of your love.

But I've gone a long way, Lord, since then.
There have been good times, strong times
when I've rejoiced in you.
Sometimes, though, the water's cold
and the swimming is hard.
It takes all my strength and I get tired,
weary, exhausted.
I'd like a rest.

You ask so much.
I'm tempted to run away, Lord,
to go into a corner and hide,
but I know you'll still be there.
And afterwards, the sour taste of failure.

So I turn and face you again, Lord.
Braced for your look of disappointment,
accusation, questioning,
and I find instead
Love.
Not soothing softness and comfort
but strength and healing.
And life.

Lord, forgive me for making the same mistakes again.
And again.
Help me to remember that when I turn to face you
I shall see your arms,
open,
in love.

Thank you.

Numbers 11:4-17

MOSES found it hard going at times leading Israel, and there were moments when he felt very inadequate. There was the occasion in the wilderness when the people were full of complaints. "Think of the food in Egypt, the free fish, the cucumbers, melons, leeks, onions and garlic. . . ." No accounting for tastes. But it hit Moses hard and you can read his reaction in Numbers chapter 11. He prays (at least he had the sense to do that with his problems!), but reading his prayer he seems to be heading straight into acute depression. "I am not able to carry this nation by myself alone, the weight is too much for me. If this is how you want to deal with me, I would rather you killed me!" He feels alone, there is no one but him to do things, no one understands or cares. He can't go on, he would be better dead, he is unworthy. God's answer, the cynic might think, would make things worse — He gives Moses a committee, and a big one too! "Gather together seventy of the elders of Israel. . . ."

The story pushes home a number of truths. First, no one is ever alone. Even while Moses is thinking that, he is talking with God — which proves the point, a point none of us should need reminding about. God is present and active in help. Then, when we feel alone and over-burdened, it is sometimes our own fault. The seventy elders had been there all the time but Moses hadn't used them; apparently he hadn't thought of sharing his responsibilities and problems with them and so, in a way, he had brought his problems on his own head. So often when we feel alone in our work it is really the limits of our own trust and vision which are the cause, not a lack of people. And may I make another point — God can work through committees! Not all committees perhaps, not the introvert, self-protective, timid groups which never make decisions; but God can share His spirit with groups of people and make them sensitive and responsive to His purposes.

I know how Moses felt, Lord.
Everything piling up,
so much to do.
I can't see the end of it.
And when that's done, there'll be more.
Spinning around,
people, places, times, voices.
Asking, demanding, expecting.

And I feel alone.
I just can't make it like this.

But then I find a moment's quiet —
like this one, Lord.
And I'm not alone anymore.
It's not that you've suddenly arrived.
You were here all the time, and I've found you again.
It's just that all those other things
got in the way,
and I was too busy.

Lord, I can see you again.

And there are others too.
Help me not to fool myself into thinking
they all need **my** help.
I'm not really so important.
Maybe it's that I want to feel needed.
Need to feel needed.
It's satisfying to think the world spins around me —
even though it's a sham.

It can be easier than asking for help.
Easier than sharing, and saying I can't do it all.

Lord, show me the joy of sharing
my problems . . . my work . . . my hopes.
Like Jesus did.
Thank you, Lord, for sharing your work with me.
Show me how to share it with others.

Mark 4:35-41

"I WILL set my face to the wind and scatter my handful of seeds on high." So says an Arabic proverb, and commenting on it, Mark Link, a Jesuit says, "My little contribution to life . . . is taken by the great wind of God and scattered where the wind wants to scatter it. . . . We need not bother too much about that part. Seeds grow. But we must have the courage to keep ourselves facing the wind."

Like all good parables, it will say different things at different times to different people. To me it says that my fulfilment must be in sowing the seed, not necessarily in hankering after the harvest. The seed is mine (although God even gave me that!) and as long as I have chosen responsibly the time and place of its scattering — and that's important — then God takes it and nurtures it to fruition. If only I could accept that more readily. Much of life's frustration comes because we expect the seedlings to come up in neat little rows exactly where we want them, but the "wind" doesn't work like that. We may see the harvest; we may not. It is, I believe, a mark of maturity that we learn to accept this, not with indifference or resignation, but joyfully and with imagination, as part of the adventure of Christian living. After all I didn't make the seed or the wind, but I can surely trust the creator to use it the way He wants to. The parable supplements the one Jesus told about planting a mustard seed, and also suggests to me a caution about our human inclination to be too proprietary about "our" things. When we actually plant something we are liable to claim it as our own, to be too protective or exclusive. Yet whether we plant it, or scatter seed in the wind, it is the Lord who brings it to maturity. How much anxiety and heartache we could avoid by accepting that, by realising that our seed sowing is much more likely to be blown about by the wind of God, than come up in the dull unimaginative ways we would expect. The most important part of the comment is that last phrase about the courage to keep ourselves facing the wind. Winds figure prominently in my experience of India — those cooling breezes with the clean smell of rain in them at the end of the hot weather, promising refreshment; and also the frightening power of the cyclone tearing down trees, halting all human movement, dramatic, destructive. It isn't always easy to face the wind, but it does keep the cobwebs down!

Lord, wouldn't it all be better
if things were organised and predictable?
If I knew the result of my actions beforehand.
If I could work out the interest on my investment
before I made it.
If I could always plant in neat little rows
and watch the seedlings grow exactly right.

I don't know if it would be better.
It would certainly be safer, and more comfortable.
Tidy.
I could work out my plans,
build my dreams, organise my life.
My plans, **my** life?

Lord, I think that's the point.
I'm looking at the world,
and the work I have to do,
as though they were mine.
But it's your world
and the only longterm plans are yours.
I can build my own ideas,
I can do what I think best and wise,
but the wind is yours too.
And it blows through my life at your will.
Sometimes it's a cool breeze
sighing through the willows by the river.
Comforting.
Sometimes it's the strong wind
hurling rain in my face
as I walk in the hills.
And it can be the screaming gale,
with purposes I don't understand.
Taking my plans and tearing them to shreds.
Or so it seems.

Lord, help me to realise
that your ways are beyond knowing.
Strengthen my faith,
that when the wind blows my world wide open
and carries the seed beyond my horizon,
I can be confident
that it will grow in other places.
And other times.
Make me see that all those other times and places
are yours too.
Lord, my job
is to keep my face to the wind.

To let it blow through my life.
Refreshing. Disturbing.
Sometimes frightening.
But always knowing that it's your wind.
And when I'm facing it
I'm facing you.

Palmtrees, Sumatra

2 Samuel 7:1-12

HAVE you noticed how God sometimes takes our hopes and prayers and, instead of giving a simple answer, reinterprets and transforms them? King David had established himself in Jerusalem after years of danger and struggle. Read the accounts in 1 and 2 Samuel. How vivid the accounts are if you use your imagination — you can feel the pressures of leadership and the strain of battle, smell the sweat and sometimes the fear, and grasp something of the whole hotchpotch of human feeling. There are so many elements in David — the striving for righteousness as he understood it, the struggle to articulate the experience of God's love and care, and its clash with those basic human drives never far below the surface — for power, or sexual fulfilment, or revenge. David, a real personality, is now settled in his walled city and the palace built for him by Hiram, King of Tyre — an early example of Foreign Aid, with fairly obvious political motives behind it! And David's thoughts turn back to God, "I'll build a temple". Men rely so much on institutions and buildings. God's people had done pretty well with the portable Ark and its curtains but now it had to be institutionalised — so David thought. But God builds people, uses people. Paul grasped this later when he described the community of believers as a body. Today humanity is at a discount. How would we put it? "We are a motor car, some are cogs, some are wheels, some spark plugs (I know a few!) others brakes (I know a few of those too!) but there is only one steering wheel." How depressing. It is *people* God uses.

David's motives seemed good. He had his house, shouldn't God have something similar? Then along comes Nathan, the prophet. God doesn't want a temple, not in David's time anyway. David must have been disappointed, resentful. When God's answer to our prayer is "No" we too are resentful. But was it a "No"? In a limited sense it was, yet in a wider sense it was to lead to a fulfilment far beyond David's understanding. Far greater than the thought of God establishing His rule through David's building of stone, the Lord promises that He will establish it through David's Kingdom and throne — forever. That's breathtaking enough, yet only with hindsight and our own experience do we now see what was impossible for David to see — that God was moving beyond a building, beyond a throne, to the kingly rule of Christ, the "Son of David". It's good to acknowledge this wider vision. Of course we plan and build and organise. These are the tools we use for our jobs, but in the changes of plan, the frustrations, the (sometimes bitter) disappointments, we need to recognise that God's plans are more glorious than we can grasp and yet, wonder of wonders, we are included in them. Soup may be "instant" but not the Kingdom of God. Many people are taken to breaking point by the strains of waiting for God's answer to their prayers, but there isn't really an alternative, is there?

Lord, it takes my breath away sometimes
when I realise that I am part of your plan
for the world.
A very small part, I know —
save me from conceit, as well as false humility —
but a part, nevertheless.
And it's good, Lord.
Good to feel not only part of your world
but also part of your plan.
Good to feel that there's something I can do
to help make your Kingdom a reality.

But help me, Lord, to remember
*that it's **your** plan not mine.*
And although I can contribute, you are in charge.
You make the decisions.
Make me content with that, Lord.

I love to tell you what I want.
I enjoy giving you the fruits of my great experience.
Sometimes I don't know how you'd manage
without the benefit of my advice!
But I have to admit, Lord, there are times when I'm stuck.
Times when I'm small and scared.
Times when I'm bewildered, when my plans come unstuck,
and I suddenly realise I don't have all the answers.
Then, Lord,
in those moments
let me remember that it's your world.
And that I don't need to have all the answers,
because you have them.
And your plans are working out.
Sometimes, it's hard to see.
Sometimes I wish you'd act more quickly
and not let things run on so.
And there I go again, telling you what to do.

Lord, it's your world.
Your plan, your time.
And beyond space and time,
greater than all my small infinities,
you are in control.
Lord, I am content.

Luke 10:38-42

I HAVE been reading a book *Letters from the Desert* by Carlo Carretto. Carretto is a monk of an Order called the Little Brothers of Jesus. It is a very "Roman" book in some ways but it is rewarding to read it quietly and receptively and let its truths speak for themselves. Before committing himself to the Order and going to live and meditate in the Algerian Desert, he had been an activist, constantly busy planning, organising, talking, doing. He writes: "For many years I had thought I was 'somebody' in the Church. I had even imagined this sacred living structure of the Church as a temple sustained by many columns, large and small, each one with the shoulder of a Christian under it. My own shoulder too I thought of as supporting a column, however small. . . . There was never enough time to get everything done. One raced continually from one project to another, from one meeting to another, from one city to another. Prayer was hurried, conversations frenzied, and one's heart in a turmoil." Then, kneeling on the desert sand one day: "I drew back suddenly, as though to free myself from this weight. What had happened? Everything remained in its place, motionless. Not a movement, not a sound. After twenty-five years I had realised that nothing was burdening my shoulders and that the column was my own creation — sham, unreal, the product of my imagination and my vanity. . . . The weight of the world was all on Christ Crucified."

Of course it isn't a licence to irresponsibility, to shrugging off our duties and not bothering what happens. But it may help to put our work and concerns into the clear perspective of God's desert light. God needs our lives, our witness and work, but His plans won't come crashing down in ruins if we fail, so we mustn't take ourselves too seriously. Maybe our particular work or interest could use more staff or more equipment — urgently, in our eyes — and our activities are hampered by the lack. But God's purposes will endure, and blossom and bring forth fruit, whatever happens to "our" schemes.

The other question is the timing. We live in an "instant" world. We can't wait any more: we want instant credit to avoid waiting while we save to buy something. It must all happen NOW. But not in God's plans. Joseph waited in prison until God's purposes matured; Moses was in the desert a long time; Jesus spent many years of life in obscurity; so did John the Baptist, and Paul. I must confess there are times when, faced with a problem, I mutter to myself, "Well, it's in the Lord's hands. He'll deal with it — but I wish He'd hurry up a bit!" But both the purpose and the timing are His, and I reckon He knows what He's doing!

To rest in you,
that's the secret, Lord.
To let go of things.
To stop worrying at them like a dog with a bone.
To acknowledge that God rules.
And that while you want me
to be concerned and committed
my failures are not going to wreck your plans.
If they survived Calvary they can survive me!

Forgive my egotism, Lord.
The feeling that it all depends on me.
That if I weren't around things wouldn't get done,
or not in the way I know is best.
Forgive me, Lord, for acting
as though everything rested on **my** shoulders.
And that nothing that is created can be created without me.
That's your privilege, Lord,
forgive me for taking it as my own.

Slow me down, Lord.
Help me to make time to wait for you.
Help me to think, to be aware.
Aware of myself.
But, more important, aware of others.
So often I fulfil **my** needs in other people.
I help them by doing what I think will be good for them
without pausing to find out what they need and feel.
There was a man who filled a whole day of my holiday
with good ideas
and with the best intentions,
without ever asking me what I wanted to do.
I do the same.
Forgive me, Lord.
Help me to know your peace and tranquillity.
Teach me that my tranquillity
can be as much a blessing to others as my activity.
Teach me that your peace
can calm and comfort.
Encourage and strengthen.
And do it in your time, Lord,
not mine.

Ecclesiastes 3:1-11

I AM sitting writing in the departure lounge of an international airport, after a busy weekend of meetings. Having to take the chance of this few minutes lends point to a phrase from a letter written to me recently. She writes, "I feel the pressure of the shortness of time...." My reaction is simple: "Don't we all!"

There is never enough time to do everything one wants to do; not even enough time to do all the things which need to be done. There is the pressure (I almost said "temptation" because I think sometimes it is just that) to lengthen work hours, relax less, and prove how indispensable one really is! That's dangerous though, not only because of Parkinson's Law — "Work expands to fill the time available" — but because the more pressure we allow on ourselves the less sure is our judgment. We become enslaved to the tyranny of the urgent, rather than free to pursue what we believe to be truly important.

And the first thing that disappears in our busyness is the personal touch. We quickly get to the point where personal interruptions are resented, rather than accepted as vital to our work. I'm not talking about time out to gossip, or the trifling interruptions which people should have the sense not to make, but about the real human contacts which keep our perspective warm and understanding. The wise writer of Ecclesiastes was right when he observed that "there is a time for everything" . . . joy or sorrow, work or leisure (Eccles. 3).

There are several things to note. First he says there is an appropriate time for everything, the implication being that there is an inappropriate time too. He also says that our work is given to us by God. In other words, it is God's work we do. He continues by saying that man cannot comprehend the whole work of God.

So what is it all saying to us? To me, it says "Look at your priorities, organise your time, do what you can, and then — leave it with the Lord". We can't see the whole mosaic. We need to realise that work is *His* and that we are His helpers; (did you get the idea it was the other way round?) and when we have honestly done what *we* can, it's up to Him.

When people get too busy I ask myself what they are trying to prove. There is usually a good deal of ego in it, and it takes humility to accept one's own limitations and vulnerability. But there is great peace in accepting that we can't do it all, and that in a very real way we don't need to!

Lord, I get so busy.
Sometimes because I want to help.
Sometimes because I can't say no.
Sometimes because I'm flattered to be asked.
And it all adds up to strain, to tiredness,
to not having two minutes to call my own.
And then comes the bad temper, the resentment.
And before long I'm hating the people who asked me.
Hating the people who want my help.
And then I feel guilty, and I hate them more.

Lord, I feel like a mouse in a treadmill.
Rushing around, faster and faster.
Getting nowhere.
And the first thing that goes out of the window
is you.
No time, Lord, sorry!
Then my family.
They should know I'm busy and not ask for my time!
And my friends.
Can't they see all the things I have to do?

Lord, it's at times like this that I need you most.
Yet you seem so far away.
Why, Lord? Where have you gone?
Then I hear it, the quiet voice . . .
. . . be still and know that I am God.
You **are** near. You have been all the time.
And I understand
that I can't hear you if I don't listen.
That I will feel alone if I don't give time to you.
Lord, I just thought so much depended on me.
I know the whole world wouldn't end if I took a break,
but it made me feel important.
I need to remember that it's your world, your work.
I'm glad to have a part in it, but it's yours, not mine.
And when I've done what I can,
I can safely leave the rest to you.

Lord, still my heart.
Help me cut down the adrenalin.
Give me your peace.

Acts 1:6-8

TALKING over a problem with someone the other day he remarked that God's watch usually seemed to be ten minutes slow! The point was that we sometimes see a problem, or even a solution — although far more people can point out a need than an effective answer — quicker than God appears to. One is tempted to think that our impatience is a product of our "instant" society, whether it is instant coffee, or anything else, but I believe it has been a human characteristic since things began. The anguished "How long, O Lord?" is not a new cry, although the anxiety and pain come afresh to anyone in a place or problem where "something needs doing, and needs doing now".

What do we do when nothing seems to be happening, and the situation is getting no better? Well, we do all we humanly and reasonably can ourselves to put things right. And then we wait! It may be hard but we are in an excellent tradition. Joseph, in prison on false charges, waited for two years; Moses spent years in the wilderness before God's call became clear; Paul had several obscure years between conversion and action; even Jesus had thirty years of preparation. . . . It isn't that God's watch is slow, or that our watches are fast, but that God's time is different in nature.

In Samuel Becket's play *Waiting for Godot* two actors, tramps, sit on a bare stage, talking as they wait. Wait for what? They don't know, the audience doesn't know, and nothing much happens. The play mirrors the despair of the existentialists. There is no meaning to life, no goal, no reality even. It isn't like that, really, because it misses one great truth — that even while we wait, even when nothing seems to be happening, God is preparing the ground. It may take Him a week (in our time), or a year, or century. It may be cold comfort in the moment of distress when we want action NOW but He is a God who acts; and a God who acts when He is ready. The waiting period is often an integral part of the plan, which couldn't mature otherwise. It may mean a pet project seems to "fail", or that life has to change direction, but so be it. Are we meant to be successful, or faithful? Does our effectiveness as Christians come from our achievements, or the quality of our being, and how we react to the waiting and to the acceptance of God's timing?

Your will be done, Lord,
on earth, as in heaven . . .
But could you speed it up a bit, Lord?
Isn't it possible to get things done
without all those periods when nothing much seems to happen?
I've been in American restaurants
where cold water and hot coffee
have to be on the table
within two minutes of a customer sitting down.
That's service. And it's good coffee too.
But when I think about it I wonder if it really helps.
All the speed. All the demand for instant service.
Maybe it gives me the wrong impression of myself.
Who am I that anyone should run around like that
to make me feel good?
Who am I that I should expect you, Lord,
to run around doing what I expect at my speed?

So what am I saying, Lord?
I'm not quite sure,
because when I see people in desperate need,
hungry children, friends with problems,
and little being done,
I still feel the impatience,
the bewilderment when nothing happens.
I wonder sometimes if you are listening at all.
But one thing I think I'm saying
is that when nothing is being done
maybe it's because I should be doing it.
It's so easy to blame you, Lord,
when you are waiting for me to act.
So much could happen without delay,
if only I actually did what your word tells me to do.
And the times when I really can do nothing,
what of those?
Then, Lord, teach me to wait.
Help me to understand that good wine matures slowly.
It can't be speeded up.
And if I drank it now it wouldn't be half as good.
And then, Lord, remind me that you **do** care.
Remind me of your love.
Remind me of all the evidence
that shows you are at work in the world,
as you have always been.
Forgive me that I need to be reminded,
but tell me again — because I forget so quickly —

the difference between instant and constant.
And if I have to choose, Lord,
between instant coffee or constant love,
I know which I'll take.

Kathmandu Temples

John 14:23-27

SOME time ago, my wife and I stood in Berlin, looking over the Wall which divides the city into West and East. We saw the armed border guards of the East German security forces watching vigilantly. In a corner on the Western side were five crosses, in memory of five men killed on various occasions as they tried to get through from the East. "In memory" is hardly the word — two were simply marked *"Unbekannt"* — "unknown". The day before we had crossed into East Berlin, through the maze of Communist checkpoints, to meet Christian leaders there. We visited a growing church held in an old factory building, and one of four Christian bookshops in East Berlin, trading openly and busily, with many Christian books for sale, including Bibles — yes, Bibles — and a number of commentaries. There are restrictions, but there is real witness and rather more freedom than we are sometimes told. We had tea in a Christian home, and prayer together.

We prayed for peace — a loaded word, with many meanings. My dictionary describes peace negatively as "freedom from war"; something external. In India, one hears Hindu priests chanting *"Shanti, shanti, shanti"* — "peace, peace, peace". The concept is much better than that in the dictionary. Peace is from within, to do with mind, heart, desires. It is still negative though — *shanti* is to control oneself, to need nothing, to desire nothing, to meet all that happens with acceptance. Essentially it is withdrawal, from tension, from the world and the demands of people.

The heavenly host promised peace on earth to the shepherds. Jesus gave it to His disciples: "Peace is my parting gift to you, my own peace, such as the world cannot give . . ." (John 14:27).

Peace — *shalom* — in the Bible is a very positive thing. It is "the harmony of a caring community informed at every point by its awareness of God" (John Taylor). It embraces the whole of life and works out in a whole network of right relationships — it is the Kingdom at work. *Shalom* grows from our closeness to God, and suffuses all our relationships and attitudes.

Shalom calls for action — blest are the peace MAKERS, says Jesus. Not the ones who relax in peace and "never do any harm", but those who create peace. It's a tall order, as those working in Berlin, Belfast or Beirut well know. That's because they begin at the wrong end — the external. We need to begin in our relationships with God, the surrender of fear and ego, and from that flows a new attitude to our fellows. When I meet folk who are critical of others, believing the worst, out of harmony, one of the things I ask myself is what does it imply about the peace in their hearts and minds? Sometimes we live like walking civil wars, in constant conflict within ourselves. Peace starts right here, in ME, not in the other person. That's what the baby in the dirty stable is all about!

Peace.
It falls off the tongue so glibly, Lord.
It's so easy to say, but not so easy to find.
We say it so often, we find it rarely.
Wherever I look, Lord, there is conflict.
Suffering. People wounded and dying.
Injured by the violence of inequality and neglect,
of hunger and poverty, and the greed that causes them.
Some dying from the bullets of war,
but more from the conflict in their hearts.
It isn't only the victim who dies,
but also the killer, little by little.
Until he's only a husk, a robot. The spark of love dead.
Life extinguished in a body still moving.
Lord, help me to see beyond the obvious.
He is guilty, the one with the gun,
but so am I.
I have no gun, but the violence of my life
the selfishness, the pride,
the fear that builds walls to protect me as I am, to keep him out,
my refusal to listen when he speaks, are violent.
It is my lack of love which drives him to the gun.
Lord, I know what you are saying.
Peace begins with me.
No, even that's wrong.
Peace begins with you, Lord. With you.
It's in you that I can find the answer to my fears,
that I can find the love which modifies and kills
my selfishness and pride.
It's in you that I can find acceptance as I am,
that I can know that I am loved and safe.
And that brings peace such as the world cannot give.
And in that peace I can move out,
taking the risks of love.
Building right relationships.
Sharing in the creation of the community which is your church.
Working with others to find understanding.
Breaking down the walls which separate us.
Offering, not glib words,
but myself.

Lord, make me an instrument of your peace.

1 John 3:13-20

SOME time ago I watched a television conversation between Dr. Una Kroll, Anglican deaconess and longtime crusader for the admission of women into the Anglican priesthood (incidentally I do wish the press would wake up to the fact that Baptists, Methodists, Presbyterians and the Salvation Army have had women ministers for decades!), and Anna Raeburn, an articulate journalist who runs an advice page in a leading women's magazine in the UK. They were talking about love. "Loving," said Anna Raeburn, "is a muscle, not a monolith", something which needs to be used and which deteriorates when it isn't. Love is a living thing which can move and change, flex and tear, which needs exercise and nurture; not a hard-edged, unyielding, unchangeable entity like a stone. And being a living thing it can be hurt.

Una Kroll knows a good deal about love and hurt. She is a compassionate person, not an abrasive campaigner, and her struggle on the priesthood issue has been damaging to her — as much through misunderstanding and prejudice as through honest disagreement. Speaking of this, and following up Anna Raeburn's remark, she said, "Yes, and it is not the winning, but the loving that matters".

It is a triumph of grace for anyone to put aside the personal hurt, the emotional need to hit back, and to go on loving in spite of the hurt. But it is also the only way for the spirit to survive. Loving and being hurt often go hand in hand — a reluctant yet fertile partnership. One of the major points of difference between the Christian way and that of both the extreme Left and Right is that to the Christian the end does not justify the means. This may sometimes make us look foolish but the means have an intrinsic value of their own — the argument may be lost, but victory comes in the loving. It is a dangerous belief because it can be used by the weak as an excuse for not fighting at all. It is dangerous too because it makes us vulnerable; there are always forces ready to hurt and kill love. But used rightly, it is the strongest weapon of all because, if the victory is in the loving, we cannot be defeated by outside forces at all. Defeat can only come from within. We may suffer hurt, but, as Calvin Miller says in his parable *The Singer* — "Love rarely ever reaches out to save except it does it with a broken hand". "By this we know what love is, that Christ laid down His life for us" (1 John 3:16). The dying was the hurt inflicted on love yet, by still loving, the defeat was turned into victory.

It's a many-splendoured thing, Lord.
Love.
So the writer says.
And we are all looking for it, one way or another.
The child running to mother, arms outstretched.
Man and woman setting up home together.
Happy in giving.
Friends sharing intimacies.
But Lord, it's so easily perverted.
Selfish parents refusing freedom
in the name of love.
Couples meshing each other in nets of frustration,
in the name of love.
Lonely men looking for instant love
through postcard phone numbers in backstreet shop windows.
Love, Lord?

I turn to you.
And I see, hear, feel what love is all about.
Love in the hand stretched out
to the paralysed man, to the leprosy sufferer, in healing.
Love offered to the corrupt tax official,
and to Mary Magdalene. In restoration.
Love in story and parable.
In rebuke.
Love in the stable.
Love on the cross.
Love forgiving as the pain of the nails
rasped through the body hanging there.
Love in the resurrection.
Offered in comfort to Mary, weeping outside the tomb.
For Peter, for doubting Thomas, for Paul the persecutor.

Love for me.
Wiping away the guilt. Drawing me near.
Standing me on my feet.
Pointing me in the right direction.
Pointing me towards others.
Love.
I can only keep it if I give it away.

Lord, help me to show your love.
Today.
For Christ's sake.

Luke 6:27-36

TURNING the other cheek has never been a popular activity, even among Christians. Outside the circle it's often labelled as weak or foolish. Yet, "Love your enemies", says Jesus, "do good to those who hate you, pray for those who . . ." (Luke 6:28-29). It doesn't come easily, or naturally. Response to a hurt is quick and instinctive. We strike back, sometimes physically or verbally; almost always mentally in the build up of resentment and anger against those who oppose or disagree with us. You'd be surprised (or would you?) how often this instinctive, un-controlled anger is the source of trouble between Christian workers — usually disguised, often unadmitted, but nonetheless real. It is common, yet disappointing and hurtful both to the cause and to us as individuals. Something I read a couple of days ago led me on to a helpful insight. The book was *Why Am I Afraid To Tell You Who I am?* an introduction into personality and counselling by John Powell, an American Jesuit. He tells of a man who bought his newspaper each day from a bad tempered salesman. In spite of daily provocation he always behaved courteously no matter how rude the other man was. "Why," asked a friend, "do you stay so pleasant and cool?" The answer came, "Why should I allow his bad temper to pull *me* down? Why should his rudeness set the lines for my behaviour?"

It seems to me that turning the other cheek is not simply a question of forgiveness, or non-violence — the usual interpretations. It is also a question of determining how far I will allow someone else to control my personality and behaviour. If I respond unpleasantly to an unpleasant person then I am allowing that person to rule my life. I am reacting to his anger and allowing myself to be pulled down to that level. If I take hold of myself and say "No . . . I'm not going to react like that . . ." then I stay a little more in control of events, and I am that little bit more mature as a person than I was before. We must go further of course, because the power to control lies not in us, but in the Spirit of God within us. As we cooperate with the Spirit in controlling those instinctive reactions we give Him a little more elbow room in which to work. And remember, controlling those reactions, that anger, only comes through admitting it, not in pretending that it doesn't exist! It isn't easy, but if I want to be ME, the mature, balanced person God wants me to be, it's the only way. The ME who responds with love and understanding each time, the ME in whom Christ can be seen.

Lord, there are times when I feel so angry!
Some word said, some action,
which makes me feel hurt or slighted.
And I respond instinctively.
I lash out in blind rage.
I want to hurt, I want to crush him,
to see him speechless, humiliated.
The harsh words, the sarcasm I label "humour",
out beyond recall before I know it.
Sometimes I say nothing.
But the anger is still there,
the words bouncing around my mind
in a nuclear explosion of rancour.
My body aches with tension, taut with grievance.
And I try to hide it, Lord.
Somehow it seems wrong to admit it, to confess my anger.
I pretend it isn't there,
I push it down into that black hole inside me
where it seethes and bubbles
and transforms itself into bitterness.
And it poisons my life.

They made you angry, Lord.
The Pharisees with their hypocrisy.
The traders bringing their dishonesty into the temple.
There's a place for it when it's not selfish.
But my anger isn't "righteous". Far from it.
Lord, I don't want it like that.
I want to be free.
I want to be in control, to weigh my words.
I want to think before I speak,
(isn't it easy to say, Lord?),
to understand before I act.
And if I understood, really understood,
maybe I wouldn't be angry at all.
Lord, I've tried. And tried again.
It's time I asked you.
I think of you before Pilate, and Herod, not opening your mouth.
I think of your cross.
No anger — just words of forgiveness — even then.

Lord, take my anger. Nail it to your cross.
And fill the space it leaves with your love.
It's a big space. It will take some filling.

Matthew 18:21-35

IT would hardly have been a hypothetical question, knowing Peter as we do — impulsive, emotional Peter. "Lord, how often am I to forgive my brother if he goes on wronging me?" (Matt. 18:21). Someone must have hurt or angered him, and more than once — ". . . if he goes on wronging me . . ." he says. Some people are relatively easy to forgive. A person with whom we have a one-off misunderstanding which leads to his apologising, the one who admits that something went wrong and pays his debt to my hurt pride. Indeed it can lead to warmer relationships all round — the nice warm glow of reconciliation, the satisfaction of having done the right thing. But there are others in my life, the aggressive, the unrepentant ones, who won't — or can't — admit they've done anything wrong. (I'm assuming of course that I've looked at the problem squarely and honestly and admitted my share of the blame!) People who provoke a slow smouldering frustration in me that builds up and breaks out in a fierce flame of resentment. What about them? Those who continue to trample on my ego and my pride, the ones who hurt me most? "Lord, how often am I to forgive?"

Jesus' answer says in effect that it's not a matter of numbers — whether seven, or seventy times seven — but of a fundamental attitude to people, and to one's self — which struggles to prevent that long term resentment from building up at all. It seems to me that the real pain — "the Cross within" — comes not from the pain of real or imagined injury, but from the pain of forgiving, the deliberate putting aside of the hard reaction, the retaliation, the cold and cutting words one would so enjoy saying. This is the forgiveness no one ever sees because it has to be deep inside, right alongside the original hurt. This I believe is the real cross we must bear — not the act of crucifixion laid on us from outside, but the cross of forgiveness which is laid on us from within.

It is what a Christian writer has described as "heart-breaking courtesy". It isn't an easily acquired gift; it needs the sort of conscious discipline we modern Christians are not very good at keeping up. We can manage the quick burst of self-abasement in the weekly prayer meeting, but this longterm schooling in the development of love is tough going. Yet that is the demand of Christ. It isn't an easy road to travel but it is the only one which leads to a fuller development of our own Christian personalities — any refusal to forgive in me damages me more than it hurts the offender. "If you love only those who love you. . . ."

Lord, I like the theory.
The idea of forgiveness.
The principle's fine:
that every time my brother upsets me
we get together and put it right.
And vice versa.
The problem is the way it works out.
Because when I get down to it, it feels different.
When I really am hurt,
When my pride's in tatters,
and I'm bruised by his big feet
trampling all over my ego
I forget about forgiveness.
I want to hit back.
I want him to know what he's done,
to feel my resentment.
I want him to know the pain he's caused.
I want him to suffer.

Lord, reading that bit back it seems full of self.
It's all about **my** feelings and needs.
Lord, forgive me.

There it is again — "forgive me".
It seems different now.
When I've made a mistake
it seems natural for me to ask for your forgiveness.
And to be confident that your love
will cover what I've done.
And I don't think too deeply
about the pain I've caused you.

Lord, did it hurt you as much to forgive me
as it does for me to forgive my brother?

I can imagine the nails,
and the agony of hanging there.
On the cross.
But I don't think that was the real agony.
The real pain was the cross inside.
The pain of rejection, the hate, the hurt.
And of forgiving those who had caused it.

Lord, forgive me.
Help me to see more clearly
the hurt I cause you.
By my resentment and pride.
Help me to look again at my brother.
At his need.

And, Lord,
give me the courage and the love
to accept the pain
of forgiveness.

Oxfordshire Farm

1 John 4:17-21

R ECENTLY, I found a book by Laurens van der Post which I'd never read — *The Night of the New Moon*. He was an officer in the British Army during World War II, and this book chronicles his experiences as a prisoner of the Japanese for several years up to 1945. Life was grim, treatment harsh. He writes:

"It was amazing how often and how many of my men would confess to me, after some ... excess worse than usual, that for the first time in their lives they had realised ... the dynamic liberating power of the first of the Crucifixion utterances: 'Forgive them for they know not what they do'.... Forgiveness became a product not of an act of will or of personal virtue even, but an automatic and all compelling consequence of a law of understanding: real and indestructible.... Forgiveness ... was not mere religious sentimentality; it was as fundamental a law of the human spirit as the law of gravity. If one broke the law of gravity one broke one's neck; if one broke this law of forgiveness one inflicted a mortal wound on one's spirit and became once again a member of the chain-gang of mere cause and effect from which life has laboured so long and painfully to escape."

This takes forgiveness and puts it firmly in place as the very basis of meaningful life. It is not optional, it is as obligatory to human growth as is water to a growing plant. To break the law of forgiveness, he says, is to injure oneself. By implication, to do it repeatedly is death — to kill that germinating seed of eternal life inside each one of us before it can break through to the full glory of light and liberation, free of the constraints put on it by the anger and resentments which come so "naturally" to us. To forgive, however painful, is to live. To harbour resentment is to remain enslaved to the circle of hurt and retaliation and more hurt which leads to the death of the spirit. To forgive is to identify with Christ, to stand with Him, to share in the fact and glory of His life, and to be freed to love. "If a man says, 'I love God', while hating his brother ..." (1 John 4:20). It is as traumatic as childbirth and just as liberating.

Lord, I want to be free
to love.
I want to be rid of all the resentment,
the anger which blocks the channel
and makes love seep away unnoticed, unused.
I read your word about love.
It almost mocks me.
You are love.
There is no fear in love.
He who loves you loves his brother also.
That's what it says.
I believe it. I hold it in my mind.
And I cry out, Lord, "make it true in my life".
Because it isn't.

It isn't the reality I know.
The reality is that each time
that little plant of love
breaks through the hard soil of my life
it gets crushed.
It struggles for life
in the barrenness of my selfishness.
There is little to water and feed it.
Because I find it hard to forgive.
And yet it breaks through again and again.

That gives me hope, Lord.
Because it's your love, your forgiveness.
Never taking no for an answer.
Never giving up on me.
Returning to the struggle again and again.
Lord, that's good.
You are only asking me to do to others
what you do to me. Constantly.
And offering me the strength to do it.

Lord, make forgiveness and love
the basis of my life.
Not in words only
but in deed and truth.
That my love for you
may show itself
in loving my brothers.

John 8:30-36

A COUPLE of days ago I watched the sunrise. It rises very late in the morning in England during autumn, so don't imagine I'd been up half the night. The morning was dark; the garden, the trees and the houses beyond hazy, and indistinct. A groundmist stretched itself lazily around them. Then the sun, large and red, began moving up the sky, penetrating the mist, disturbing it, giving form and clarity to things so dimly seen. I turned to my reading. John 8:31 caught my attention: "You shall know the truth, and the truth will set you free."

There seemed a very simple connection between the words and the sunrise; the mist dispersed, the hazy halflight made clear and bright by the honey touch of the sun. But it isn't quite as simple as that, not always so idyllic and beautiful. The sun is a flame. It burns; and so can truth. It is this purifying, penetrating side of truth which we need to take more to ourselves. We sometimes shrink from the truth because it hurts. Do you remember the last time you skirted round the real truth in a conversation because the truth was unpalatable, and you didn't want anyone to feel hurt? And then later you wished that you had faced up to it?

Laurens van der Post, that sensitive and profound author from South Africa, writes: "Truth, however terrible, carries within itself its own strange comfort for the misery it is so often compelled to inflict on behalf of life. Sooner or later it is not pretence but the truth which gives back with both hands what it has taken away with one."

Yes, sharing the truth with someone can be painful, but shared openly and in love, it carries its own healing with it, in its own time. The qualifying phrase of course is "in love". Don't go rushing out in the strength of these words to spill out those resentments you've built up over a colleague, but do learn to "share the truth in love". Finally, can you take the truth in love when it is offered to you? That's the hardest thing, but freedom in Christ comes only by facing up to the truth about oneself. That is something no colleague can tell you or me, only the Holy Spirit working in us.

Start with me, Lord.
I like the idea of being more truthful,
of being honest with people.
Telling them when I'm hurt or irritated
by something they've done.
I like the idea of helping others —
in love of course, Lord —
to see their faults and come to terms with them.
I know I'll have to pick my words carefully,
that it won't be easy . . .
The problem is that they may do it back to me.
I'm not so sure about that.
It's not that I don't have faults, I know I do,
and I know something has to be done about them.
But they aren't always easy to face . . .

Lord, I don't even think I'm being honest now!
If I were, I'd admit that the truth —
the whole truth — is never easy.
It frightens me.
It's not just the honey touch of the sun,
it's a living flame.
Because the truth has to begin with me,
not with other people.
I've got to start peeling away my own defences.
I've got to look at myself in the strong light of Your truth.
That's painful, Lord.
The nerve endings are raw and sensitive.
Because there's not much there worth looking at.
There's a whole ragbag of emotion and prejudice and fear
and I'd rather not look.
But maybe that's the point.
If you can help me to see what I am, warts and all,
maybe I won't feel the urge to criticise others quite so much.
I might have a little more patience,
maybe even begin to understand.

And there's another thing.
I know you love me — I don't know why, but you do.
And if you can find something loveable in me,
maybe I can see the same in the people I work with,
because you love them too.
That gives me a starting point in my relationships.
It means I don't start with the faults,
but with love.

So when I do have to share my feelings and criticisms with others
let it begin with love.

Take that rasp out of my voice,
the tension out of my body,
the aggression out of my mind.
It's not easy, but you know that Lord.
You must have come to terms with yourself in the wilderness,
so you know the way I feel.
I'm still scared.
I can only face the truth about myself a bit at a time,
but I know now that that's where I have to begin.
Lord, start with me . . .

Hindu Temple, South India

Galatians 2:17-21

IN cynical moments I've thought that a useful yardstick for measuring freedom in a country would be to count the references to it in the media: the more references there are, the less freedom there really is! It often seems that the people who shout most about freedom are those who really wish to enforce their own views on everyone else. In other words, to enslave.

St. Paul insists that "Christ set us free, to be free men" (Galatians 5:1), and in the New English Bible the whole letter is headed "Faith and Freedom". The Galatians were a subject people under the restrictions of the Roman Empire, its administration firm, its laws harsh to wrongdoers. Paul's freedom was the freedom faith brings, the Christian paradox, true nonetheless, the freedom of the spirit totally independent of outside conditions. The freedom even a slave can experience! And if I had to put my Christian experience into one word I would say "Freedom", because it embraces everything else, the forgiveness, rehabilitation, salvation, the adventure of change, the new relationships which become possible.

The sad thing is to see Christians, at times, progress backwards! From the liberating experience of personal commitment to Christ, with the joy and freedom He brings, back to the slavery of doing things because "people expect it". This is the very thing Paul fights fiercely in his letter. Then it was circumcision, today a host of traditions and attitudes which are so often and wrongly equated with Biblical truth. A thing I covet for young Christians is the freedom to be themselves, to develop their own personalities rather than the "image" they think is expected of them, the courage to resist those who try to pigeonhole them, and the understanding which resists the temptation to pigeonhole and judge others.

Jesus' coming to earth fitted no pattern. Christmas was unconventional. God in man, King in a stable, power in weakness, God's glory in a deprived baby on the edge of the Third World. God doing things in the way His wisdom says is best, whatever orthodox reaction may be, to bring us freedom. Freedom in Christ, freedom to love and to live as He wants you to. Freedom in His service.

I watched him, Lord, the hawk.
Holding height on quivering wings, using the flow of air.
Then a swoop, a side slip and a glide
slicing deep into the singing wind.
Free.
Yet not free. Ruled by instinct.
Conditioned by needs — food, sex, self preservation.
A whole bundle of unconscious energies.

Not that freedom, Lord.
Freedom in Christ is different.
Free to understand the world and self in a different light.
Free from the fears and guilt which hold me down.
Free, in your forgiveness and strength
to take new values and ideals.
Free to a new hope and a new life.
Free to love others rather than myself.
Free to respond to their needs, not just to my own.

Freedom can be selfish.
Teach me, Lord, in my freedom,
not to trespass on the rights of others.
It's so easy.
I want them to share what I've got,
to know the joy, to feel the wind.
But when I speak, as I live my life,
help me to respect their freedom.
Their right to choose, to be different.
Being different isn't always wrong.
After all, I'm different!
That's part of the glory of your creation, Lord,
that you've made us so diverse.
And when the Spirit takes us and starts to rebuild us
we don't all have to come out alike.
It's not a Ford production line
— and even that has different models —
but life.
Thank you, Lord, for making us different.
And thankyou, Lord, because you love each one of us.
And because, whoever we are, you can use us.

Philippians 3:7-14

"HAVE you left home yet?" The question was asked by a speaker at a Christian Conference. It's a good question. Most of the people he was speaking to had certainly left home geographically. They were living and working in different countries far away from home. But, as Teilhard de Chardin once remarked, that doesn't necessarily mean we've moved at all. We can travel around the world without changing our basic position one centimetre. "Home" is not so much a place as a way of life. "Home" is habits, beliefs, prejudices, fixed ways of thinking and doing.

If we want God to work on us and in us then we have to leave home and go on pilgrimage with Him. There is no other way but out into the unknown. That's what Abraham did, and his traumatic experience was not in swapping one bit of desert for another but in leaving the safety of a "local" God and moving into the vastness of the experience of a universal God. Often the pilgrimage is hindered by our home attitudes. Did Jesus have this in mind when He said ". . . unless you leave home and kindred. . . ."? Not that He devalued loving relationships but that He understood how fixed ways of thinking could chain one's spirit.

The only way to freedom is to allow the chains to be broken — the habits, the refusal to consider other ways. Freedom is for the brave, and it is the timid, defensive Christian who refuses new experiences and thought, and clings to "home". I've known missionaries who have worked in a country for 20 years but who have never really *lived* there, and never become a real part of the local community because they cannot open themselves to new ideas or thoughts. The way we walk with Jesus isn't geographical, it is a totally new life style, a new way of being. This is the point for all of us. In Christian terms it isn't the expertise we bring, the way we do the job, or handle people (although these are important), but whether the living Christ is within us. That's what people need to see in us: a new creation, a new being, men and women freed from fear, suspicion, prejudice. Liberated from "home" to be explorers, travelling joyfully and freely, not in a jet, but in the Spirit.

Lord, I thank you for home.
For those I love, and those who love me.
For family, and friends.
For community and fellow workers.
For those who give me a sense of worth and purpose.
For all in life that strengthens me,
and helps me face people with confidence.

Yet sometimes, Lord, I cling to these things too much.
My life gets cluttered up with custom and repetition.
I hold hard on habit.
It's easier to do things the same old way.
I practise religion, not faith.
My attitudes are formed more by prejudice than understanding.
It's comfortable. I don't have to think.
But you call me to more than that.
Jesus stands at the door.
Knocking, to come in?
Yes, but also asking me to come out.
Holding open a door to new horizons.
Unknown, limited only by my courage.
Showing me the Kingdoms of **his** world.
Offering the joy of pilgrimage,
of walking out, free, with him.
Liberation.
From fear.
From all the anxieties and suspicions
which hem my life around and breed new fears.
Liberation, because he is with me.
Wherever I go.
Freedom, not from responsibility and obligation,
but freedom from self.
Freedom from all that holds me back
from giving my love, myself, to others.

The road stretches out, and as I take one step,
and two, the road moves on.
No end in sight. Just new horizons.
But you are there, taking the steps as I take them.
Sharing the adventure.

Lord, it's risky. There's so much space.
But the real shelter is not in the walls I build.
It's in you.

Matthew 16:13-23

"YOU are the Messiah, the Son of the Living God," said Peter. And immediately Jesus began to teach the disciples that the path ahead was one of suffering. Peter didn't like the idea one little bit; he was ready for anything, but not that!

I am convinced of the reality of Christian joy, and how I long for it to be more in evidence within Christian communities, but the fact that it is not always present goes back perhaps to the difficulty we share with Peter: the problem of accepting the reality of suffering too. The Christian Church is a community — a community of fellowship, a caring community, and a suffering community. Deeper fellowship comes, not through better organisation (although we need that for other reasons) but through sharing in Christ's suffering and death.

The basic thought came back to me again the other day as I read a quote from Monica Furlong, who writes of: ". . . one shattering insight that the heart of human experience properly lived, is death, but that this death faithfully experienced, inevitably yields again to life."

Yes, we assent to it because the theologians tell us it is so; but we still find it hard to accept its reality in our own experience. But Jesus made it real and each little death we die, in daily living, brings real life, and it is in this that the suffering and the joy come together. As we defer to each other in love, rather than to self; as we stand with people in their suffering; as we walk daily with Jesus on our own Jerusalem road the Holy Spirit becomes real to us, we feel His presence, we experience His power — and His joy comes true. John Taylor, if I can be allowed to paraphrase him, suggests that the action and the presence of the Holy Spirit is seen in woundprints. That's worth thinking about. The Church is not simply an organisation with specific aims and goals, not just a well or badly run machine, but the body of Christ; and that's where the woundprints are.

Does it really have to be that way, Lord?
Can't you make it simpler?
One minute it's joy, the next it's suffering.
It's not that I can't understand,
it's that I don't really want to.

I'm all for the joy —
the fellowship of friends, the satisfaction of service,
the singing and the hallelujahs (not too loud, though!) —
but not the suffering.
"Not for you, Lord" said Peter.
And maybe under his breath he added
"Nor me. . . ."
It comes hard, the suffering.
When I said I'd give up everything, Lord,
I didn't really think it would be like this.
I didn't really think it through.
Yet it's true, I know it is.
Forgive me for trying to sidestep,
but it hurts.
Little deaths every day.
Choking back the angry word,
not telling the other driver he's a bloody fool.
Responding with love.
Giving, not receiving.
Giving a bit more when no one says Thank you
for what I've already given.
Giving my time, and energy, and help,
when all I want to do
is curl up on my own.

Then I look at you, Lord, and I'm ashamed.
I see the wounds.
Not just on your hands and feet,
but in your heart.
And I know there's no other way.
Your death brought life.
In dying you live.
In your life I too am alive.
And your life grows in me
through all these little deaths I die each day.
And through them you bring me closer
to yourself.
Lord, I don't really want it any other way.

Philippians 1:3-11

PAUL'S experience was that faith and hardship often complement each other in the Christian life. Because of it one might expect Paul to have a rather sombre approach to life; a sort of "grin and bear it" attitude, dogged and dour. Not so, Paul was much more positive. His life was studded with problems, but it was also filled with joy. It wasn't a spasmodic joy which came in the pauses between the problems, like a sort of spiritual serendipity, but a deep-rooted joy which carried him through the hard times with strength and resilience. Look at his letter to Christians at Philippi: "... when I pray for you all, my prayers are always joyful ..." (Phil. 1:4).

Always. There are two points worth making. First, Paul's joy in the Philippians didn't come because they were a lovely crowd of happy, co-operative Christians — they weren't. Read the letter, and read between the lines. Paul writes of the need for unity and stresses that there should be no rivalry or vanity among them. We can reasonably assume that there was need for his writing in that way, or why bother? So Paul is dealing with the same sort of fallible human beings we have to deal with today. Paul looks beyond their faults though, and sees the good and the potential for good there was in them. They are his partners in the Gospel, fellow workers and, just as he experiences the Holy Spirit at work in his own life, he has the sensitivity and humility to accept that the same Spirit is working in them, bringing to completion the good work already begun in them. Paul doesn't patronise them, but sees them as co-workers, imperfect like himself, but people for whom Christ died, and people in whom Christ is working.

Second, look at the physical context of Paul's joy. He is writing from prison — not a place geared to generate joy. Yet rejoice I will, affirms Paul, whatever happens. His joy is not at the mercy of superficialities, changing like the wind, but arises from his confidence in the support of the Spirit, and in his experience of the strengthening which their prayers for him gave. The Christian's faith is unfair to the non-believer! It depends on experience, not on theory. If you've not got the experience you can't have the joy; if you've once experienced the joy Paul writes of, nothing can take it away! Yes it's a difficult, 'ornery world, and people can be difficult too; but God is at work in the world, prayer is abroad, and Paul is content to know that he is within God's purposes. Come what may, he will rejoice, because he is not alone.

Always *joyful, Lord?*
It's not easy to accept,
but it is written down there.
I just have to try to work it out.
First, joy in people.
Not that they were perfect, those "saints" in Philippi.
Just ordinary Christians, like me,
like the ones who stand in the pews
and sing with me on Sunday.
Folk who gather, not because they're good
but because they know their need of you.
Still struggling with their personalities.
Still doing the things they don't want to do.
Finding it hard to do the right things.

Lord, help me to rejoice in the people I know.
They aren't perfect, but neither am I.
Pigheaded, stubborn, timid and aggressive by turn,
but also kind and helpful.
Loving when I need them.
Willing to give a hand when I go down.
And when I open my eyes I can see you in them.
You, leading them — and me, Lord, **and** *me –*
slowly, sometimes painfully,
but with infinite love and understanding
to a deeper knowledge of yourself.
And there's the joy, because we are pilgrims.
Together. With you.

But joyful in prison, Lord? Honestly?
Was Paul really able to forget where he was,
to ignore the confinement, the restrictions and frustrations,
and laugh?
No, Lord, it wasn't as superficial as that.
It was your presence, Lord, and his confidence in you.
You'd never let him down.
He'd been bullied, and flogged, laughed at and cursed,
left half dead,
but you were always there.
Not only strengthening him, but suffering with him.
Holding him up. Leading him on.
Loving him.
And with you there
the places and conditions don't matter quite so much.
Lord, let me know you near, as Paul did.
Let me know, beyond doubt, that you will never go away.
And whether things are easy or tough

let me know through my laughter and tears
that you are with me.

And there's the joy.

Sussex Landscape

Luke 9:28-45

SOME people can walk quietly and calmly into a situation of confusion, size it up, and do something about it. It's a rare and enviable gift, and Jesus had it. Read Luke 9:28-45, and immerse yourself in the atmosphere. After the exaltation of the experience on the mountain and the peace of the night in the hills, Jesus was met by a crowd of people. It was a large and curious crowd, shoving and elbowing, closing in, talking, quarrelling, dirty and sweaty, staring at the Galilean prophet they had come to see. In the middle of it comes a shouted protest, a criticism of the way His disciples were handling things. "Look at my son, your disciples couldn't do anything." Crowd, noise, heat, criticism, sickness. The disciples helpless, the father disappointed, belligerent. To make it worse the boy goes into convulsions. In it all, Jesus is competent, and in control of the situation, effectively translating the love of God into action, by healing the boy and restoring him to the father.

Jesus was firmly in control of His own reactions too. Surrounded by wonder and admiration for what He had done, He gently takes His disciples beyond the immediate, beyond the healing, quietly revealing the fundamental purpose of His presence with them, leading them gently up to the cross. Not carried away by success, He shared His compassion in full understanding of where it would lead Him.

Lord, you were always in control,
whatever faced you.
Human need, suffering and pain.
Poverty and hunger.
Doubt and disbelief.
Anger and hate.
The cynicism which says good is evil,
and twists motives beyond belief.

And when people came,
anxious, frightened, angry people,
not knowing which way to go,
you were ready for them.
Offering love, strength,
understanding, comfort, challenge.
Above all, love.

In control, because you saw beyond the immediate.
Because your Father's purposes
were clear, and real.
Because everything was subordinate to that.
And always,
in responding to pain and need,
you pointed people onwards,
beyond the hurt,
to the love that never lets us go.

Lord, when I'm faced with crisis,
with demands on time and attention,
when the fingers of panic start to churn
and I can't cope,
Lord, let me take your hand.
Help me to see your eternal purposes
within the demands of daily living.
Show me the essential beyond the immediate.
And protect me from being so busy with the urgent
that I have no time for the important.

And, Lord, give me your peace.

Matthew 16:24-28

IT was painted on the blank wall outside a supermarket, facing the car park. "You are only as rich as the things you can do without." Very true, I thought. I pictured the painter as a frustrated shopper, worried by more price increases and intent on cutting down the family's cost of living. First, the protest; then burn her car; then retire to the simple life on a mountain top. Very good — here was someone grasping for a real assessment of the things which so much of the world values. But then I came to the point of realising that, like so many catchy slogans, it was only a half truth, pointing up the superficiality of our thoughts, and proving the poverty of our reliance on material things. The slogan writer was protesting about materialism, but apparently able to conceive of poverty and riches only in the material terms he or she was rebelling against.

My fingers itched to put up another daub alongside: "You are only as rich as the things you possess," and to work this out, not in the material context of the first slogan but in the Christian's experience of the riches of Christ who "... for your sake became poor, so that through his poverty you might become rich" (2 Cor. 8:9). What are those riches? "Christ in you, the hope of a glory to come" (Col. 1:27).

Our true riches lie, not in the acceptance or rejection of the material as though nothing else existed, but in our ready acceptance of the spiritual, and in the possession of a continuing experience of the presence and power of the Holy Spirit. Rich, not in the ephemera of the supermarket, but in those things "which the world cannot give" — love, joy and peace.

Lord, I'm rich.
I'm rich because you love me, and I know it.
Rich beyond anything the world can give.
Rich because the world can't take it away.
It's there, your love, and nothing I do will change it.
I can reject it, forget it,
but it's still there.
I only have to reach out and it's mine.

I'm rich because of faith.
Because, knowing your love, I can believe the rest.
When I'm down, things get unreal.
Disconnected.
It's so easy to question,
to hang my insecurity on to you.
To blame you for my own weakness,
to say there's something wrong with the system
when I know it's me.
And then your love takes over again,
and the joy bursts out.
Like living grass through dead concrete.

I'm rich because of hope.
Because your love gives me a new perspective on life.
I may get tired and disappointed.
Things go wrong,
and I wonder what it's all about.
Then I reach out and feel that love again.
And I know that beyond the disappointment,
beyond the cares, you are there.
Always.
And my hope is real, it can't be taken away.
I may give it up, but it can't be taken away.

Yes, Lord, I'm rich,
and it has nothing to do with supermarkets.
It's not baked beans,
or this week's special offer, it's you.

You, Lord, your love, and joy, and peace.

Acts 16:16-34

PAUL must have been crazy! He and Silas had been stripped and flogged, then chained and left in a prison cell, all because they had healed a demented girl. Wrongfully arrested, stiff and bloody, every muscle-twitch painful, they must have longed for sleep. I saw a television programme recently on conditions in prison today. Physical conditions are rather different I hope, but one ex-convict said the thing he couldn't forget was the sound of men sobbing in the night, sometimes awake, sometimes asleep. Yet the sound of crying is less surprising than what was heard in the jail at Philippi that night. "About midnight Paul and Silas, at their prayers, were singing praises to God" (Acts 16:25).

Prayer was to be expected — many people pray when they are in trouble. "God, get me out of this, please," turning in helplessness to a power which may take them out of danger. A sort of "Mummy, kiss it better, please". But singing praises! I doubt if their voices were very musical as they slumped in the dark, but praise it was.

I wonder about the reactions of the other prisoners who heard them. "Go to sleep." "Shut up!" "What can you expect from roadside preachers? They're always mad!" "Maybe they got hit on the head when they were beaten up." Perhaps one or two began to question, and think. . . . The jailor did, after the earthquake. The story is tantalizingly brief, it leaves out so much. There must have been so much more to the exchange between Paul and the jailor — the expressions, the jailor's quick blurting out of questions in the flickering light, the tension, Paul's quiet, confident, compassionate replies. The behaviour of Paul and Silas brought him to Christ, together with his whole family. Later Paul wrote to these same Philippian Christians about his joy in them. "I thank my God whenever I think of you," he wrote. Paul was writing from prison in Rome, to Christians (including the jailor?) he had met in Philippi. Could he think of Philippi without remembering the beating and the jail? Yet it's a story of praise and joy.

It's so easy to say it in a facile, hollow way, yet it has to be true. Paul was so confident that God was in control that he could take life as it came. I talk to so many folk, young and not so young, who want to be sure that they are doing what God wants them to do. Sometimes it is easy and obvious, at other times it is not at all clear. In those times I believe firmly that you do what Paul did — you carry on where you are and relax in the knowledge that God is alive, awake and active; and you wait for a door to open. It may not come in one night, and it may not take an earthquake to do it but, who knows, there might be more useful earthquakes if our praise and joy was as constant and rich as Paul's. Do what he did — relax, let God take over. God rules, O.K.?

Lord, thank you.
Thank you because no one can really chain me up.
I see Paul and Silas in prison.
I hear the door, that heavy door,
thud
as it closes, and locks.
I feel the darkness, the stone walls,
I hear the rough voice asking who they are.
That was real, but so was the freedom.
They could still reach out and touch your face.
Your love, piercing walls of stone,
the walls of bruised and weary flesh, was still there.
Creative, active, breathing new life.
Renewing hope.
Renewing? but it had never left them
or grown old, or cold.
And in Paul and Silas the hope welled up, and overflowed, in praise.
Lord, thank you, because wherever I go today
you are with me.
No place is too difficult for you.
In the joys, in the pain, at work, at home, you are there.
Help me to feel you, to remember you in the good times,
as I call for you in the bad.
Sometimes, Lord, things get in the way. And you seem distant.
That hurts me, Lord, and I cry out
"Where are you? Where have you gone?"
But when I tunnel through my pre-occupations,
when I put aside the panic, you are still there.
Thank you, Lord.
But, Lord, I pray for those who are shut up in prison.
Caged in the prisons of their minds.
Bound by disbelief, or prejudice.
Unable to break free from the weight of daily life.
Immersed in ego, relating everything to self.
The insecure, shut up in fear,
to whom change, and the demands of other people
are threats, to be fought and resisted.
I pray for those who are bound
in the chains of religion.
For whom life is a treadmill of observance.
Lord, help us all
to open our hearts to the freedom you bring.
Break down the walls, Lord. Expand our horizons.
Open our eyes to your love,
our consciousness to your presence.
And the joy will come, Lord. And the praise.

1 John 1:5-10

ONE of the biggest problems in our Christian lives is our dishonesty. I will now hide under my desk until it is safe to reappear!

It's really a matter of how we see ourselves, the roles we play, and how clearly we face up to reality. Some Christians seem to believe that their witness depends on being ever hopeful, optimistic and victorious; and that to confess to moments of despair, doubt or unhappiness is somehow to be unfaithful. Yet it doesn't really fit the facts of experience. We have our "highs", the times of exaltation and spiritual uplift, and we have our "lows" too, the times when we are dry and prayer is an effort. Then we have to hang on to our faith and to the memory of earlier joys. This is part of our humanity: we should see it as such, and have the honesty to accept it. The Bible is totally honest in its recording of the ups and downs of human experience. At times Moses knew despair in leading Israel. There are many Psalms which describe the depths of loneliness and despair which the Psalmist experienced. Jesus Himself knew it.

The first thing in dealing with these times is to admit their reality. Otherwise tensions are created through playing a role which is not real. We pretend to victory and assurance, but we live a lie which can't be sustained. Fears mount, we feel guilty, and our relationships with people suffer. We need to be able to share our disappointments and fears as well as our joys — not to wallow in tears, but to face them and deal with them. Correction! When we face them the Spirit can deal with them.

And in facing the truth, in seeing ourselves as we really are — and accepting it — we can rely on the fact that Christ accepts us that way too. Then together, in honesty, we can build. I remember some years ago when I suddenly saw, sharp-edged and crystal-clear, that He loved me as I was, that I need not pretend, that I could relax — not relax my working efforts, but relax deep down and let Him take the strain.

Lord, I don't have to pretend.
Not with you.
There really isn't any point in trying to
because you know me
better than I know myself.
You know all there is of me.
The hopes,
the joys that come bubbling out when I'm feeling good.
The disappointments and failures I try to hide
to keep up appearances.
The murkiness and mud down there in my subconscious.
I like to pretend it isn't there at all
but it swirls and drifts up to the surface,
polluting the open beaches of my life
like oil patches floating in on the tide.

Yet you still love me, Lord.
I don't know why, the reasons don't matter.
Theologians may explain it
but I feel it, and I rejoice.

And because you love me, I can be honest.
I can admit the failures, the frustration,
all the things that tie me into knots of pain
and make me cry out in anger and hate,
and shame.

And because I bring them to you
you can deal with them.
With me.

It's such a relief, being honest with you.
To lose the fear, to know that my honesty
doesn't push us apart
but brings us nearer.
Because I am loved.
I belong.
I have a value which no one can take away
because you love me.
With all my faults.

Romans 12:1-10

ONE day, medical history will be made when I write a monograph on Photographer's Syndrome. It is a disease recognised by an elevated shoulder (from the weight of the camera bag), a perpetually bent and twitching forefinger, and square vision. Once infected there is no cure, other than total withdrawal of all spare cash; no cell-mediated immunity, nothing. I've had it for years, and I've just bought a new toy — a 28mm wide-angle lens for my Pentax. I've had wide-angle lenses before, but this is wider, and more expensive, than earlier ones.

Its main characteristic is both a virtue and a fault, depending on how you use it — it changes natural perspective, and makes very dramatic pictures when used creatively. You can produce large heads on small bodies, you can make eyes large and brilliant in a close-up portrait, or give a foreground object much more prominence in a picture than it really has. Who says the camera can't lie? The lens' basic use though is to give a broad picture in a tight place where a standard lens doesn't see enough. Other lenses change things too. A long-focus lens brings distant objects close; a close-up lens fills the picture with detail of one small flower.

Playing with my new lens to get used to it set me thinking about perspective in our lives and work. What do we focus on when we run into conflict with others? What perspective do we use? There are times when several people get involved in a problem. Not only do opinions differ, and the interpretation of the facts, but the facts themselves seem to change. No one wants to mislead, or grind a particular axe, but everything looks different to them. What are the focal lengths of the lenses we are using? A wide-angled view brings in many peripheral objects, the close-up vision sees detail but only in a limited field. You get the point, I'm sure. Each lens is true to its own design, but through its own perspective sees things differently.

Confronted with a picture, a perspective, different from yours, what do you do? Do you wish everyone saw things the same, or do you recognise that another viewpoint may be as true, as valid, even better than your own? Try and look through the other lens. It can be dangerous because you may begin to sympathise and see the other point of view! Do you have "difficult" colleagues, "uncooperative" workmates, perhaps "obtuse" seniors? I'm in danger of over-simplifying, but often conflict is not a question of absolutes, but of perspective, of learning to see things as someone else sees them, and sitting where he sits, accepting the fact that he may have something valid to say: "in honour preferring one another..." (Rom. 12:10). Read the words immediately before those: "In love of the brethren be tenderly affectioned one to another." That's where understanding comes from, and if love doesn't temper our conflicts, we still have a long way to go.

Conflict.
Fear.
Anger.
So often, Lord, so often.
It was only a small thing.
But it looked large,
the way I saw it,
and it frightened me.
I'm even more frightened by my reaction to it.

Lord, your world is a beautiful world,
full of beautiful people.
Yet somehow the image gets distorted.
Out of perspective.
Problems get magnified, exaggerated.
Suspicion instead of trust,
secrecy instead of openness,
jealousy in place of appreciation.
Anger where love should be.

Lord, keep my vision clear,
the lens unclouded by distrust and fear.
Keep me open to your light
that I may walk in it, and not in darkness — with joy.
Help me to respond to others
and not to distort their needs
into threats to me.

As I pray for myself
I pray for others who face disputes,
who make decisions, and who try to make peace.
Give them understanding of other viewpoints, Lord.
Not to make them indecisive and unsure,
but so that decisions can be made from knowledge.
Give the ability to see the whole,
the wisdom to concentrate on the essential.
And above all, Lord, give us loving kindness
in our judgements.

1 Corinthians 1:25-31

LIFE'S a funny thing. It runs smoothly for a bit, things seem to be going right, the rut gets comfortable, and then — Bang! Things go wrong. Not everything — although it may feel like it, and it seems as though there are problems everywhere. Really, it's a natural part of life. Not that problems are welcome; but to face them without resentment leaves us free to deal with them, rather than getting all hung up with frustration.

Most of our problems are caused by people. Computers make mistakes, but they don't have hysterics over the way a fellow computer behaves — not the way we do! And problems with people may mean problems with close colleagues. Looking back on my life in a Christian leprosy hospital in India it was a very happy and fulfilling time. But even though we worked well together there were times of tension and disagreement. Times when I said — or thought, anyway — "How can God possibly work through people like these!" And I'm sure others said the same about me. The amazing and encouraging fact is that He did and does.

Remember Paul's words "My brothers, think what sort of people you (we) are, whom God has called . . . few . . . are men of wisdom. . . . Yet God has chosen the weak and . . . the foolish . . ." (1 Cor. 1:25-30). God works through us. It may not seem a very bright idea for God to do things that way, but He's chosen it! Of course, the fact that He uses us doesn't mean we can be content with what we are; there's great danger in thinking that God must take us "as is". Not so. Jesus says "Be ye perfect . . ." or as the NEB puts it ". . . You must be all goodness . . ." (Matt. 5:48). And that doesn't just happen, we have to work at it, and that includes working at relationships with our fellow workers. Fortunately, the Lord doesn't wait for perfection. Look at the early disciples — Thomas and his doubts, Peter, impulsive and naive, John and James looking for the best places in the Kingdom.

And so it is with us. Paul had the right idea. In writing those words to the church at Corinth he's saying "You may be very imperfect but God has chosen you." God made the choice. "You did not choose me," said Jesus to His followers, "I chose you" (John 15:16). The point I want to make is this — God chooses me in my weakness, not through any virtue I possess but because He loves me. *And that goes for my colleagues too — and yours.* If God can put up with our faults then maybe we should make a better attempt to accept theirs, and to work with them as they are. Sometimes I feel we demand from our friends a perfection which even the Lord doesn't ask.

Finally, it's significant for me that Christ sandwiches the phrase about "I have chosen you" between two exhortations to love one another. I suggest that Jesus is saying "If I can love you enough to choose you for my work, then you can learn to love each other." Not just mutual tolerance — although that's a start — but loving, as Christ loved you.

Lord, it takes my breath away.
The whole idea
that you choose to work
through ordinary people like me.
I wouldn't have done it that way.
Not if I'd been in on the planning.
There's so much at stake.
There must have been other ways you could have chosen.
Ways that didn't involve ordinary people like me.

Not that I don't appreciate it, Lord.
It's just that I can see my own weakness.
And while I'm happy to help — most of the time, anyway —
I can see the problems it causes.
I see the weakness in other people too.
In fact I spend longer looking at their faults
than I do at my own.
And I don't really believe it's because
they have more faults than I have.
Simply that I see them more clearly.
Or do I?

I'm going off at a tangent, Lord,
I enjoy analysing other people.
What I'm really trying to say is this —
That when I face you,
when I think of your love,
and patience, and trust in allowing me
to share in the work of your Kingdom,
I can only say thank you, Lord.
I don't know why you take so much trouble with me,
but I'm glad you do.
And in using me
at least you are showing
that your love and your Kingdom
are for ordinary people like me.
And like my brother here . . .

Lord, when I'm tempted to criticise other people,
the one at the next desk,
the one in the pew in front of me,
when I'm tempted to question their credentials
and doubt their ability,
remind me that I'm no more than average anyway.
And Lord, if you can accept me,
and use me,
then maybe I can accept the people I have to work with.

And acknowledge
that if you choose to work through me,
then you can work through them too.
Lord, teach me to respect them more.
And help that respect to grow
into love.

Welsh Cottage.

Ephesians 6:10-13

"I DON'T know how long I can carry on in this situation. There are always problems — if they'd just leave me alone to get on quietly, I'd be alright." It's a natural thing to hope for a quiet life and yet it is the one thing a Christian can't expect. From time to time, in conversation or in letters from friends and colleagues around the world, the same cry of frustration comes. It's not always crystallised in words, but it comes through clearly and recognisably, underlying attitudes and comment. We find life more difficult than we expected. There is opposition, criticism of what we are trying to do. Is it worthwhile going on? Another person protests that "We shouldn't have to face this sort of problem in Christian service!"

Now don't read too much into this — my life isn't totally occupied dealing with agonised cries from people with problems — far from it! But there are enough folk in difficult situations to give real thought to them.

First, let's put it in perspective. It isn't new to have problems; and if it happens to you, don't think you are unique. There was Paul, 1900 years ago, appealing to Christians at Thessalonica ". . . to stand firm for the faith, and, under all these hardships, not to be shaken ... we warned you that we were bound to suffer hardship; and so it has turned out . . ." (1 Thess. 3:3-5).

Faith and hardship, writes Paul, go together. Not always, in my experience, but often. It happened in Thessalonica, and it happens today, wherever Christians are seeking to live lives of loving service and witness. It happens because the Christian life sets us clearly at odds with much of the world, and we must expect opposition. So don't be surprised when discouragement comes, realise that faith and hardship may go together and cling to the recollection of good things.

Perhaps part of the problem is that the opposition comes from sources we don't expect. Difficulties may come from within our work, not from outside. Hard-headed, square-cornered colleagues, critical co-workers. Wherever it comes from our witness depends on how we take it.

One other thing — we all get it! In moments of stress we are tempted to say there is no point in going on — "It just isn't worth it" — because God can't work in our particular situation. Really? Do we believe in a God with limited power? Somehow, that's not my reading of the New Testament (or of the Old for that matter!). What I see, and know from experience, is a God who constantly surprises me by working through "impossible" situations, in ways I don't understand and in ways I don't expect. But He continues to do it; a God who can strengthen us to face our problems, where we are, without flinching. Of course we shall have problems; we have no right to expect otherwise, and maturity includes the recognition of this fact, but we face them with God, we face them together, and we strengthen one another with prayer.

Lord, you are the God of the impossible.
Your power and wisdom are infinite.
Your understanding reaches through the far horizons of space,
and down into the secret crevices of my mind.
The universe is not too large for you,
the atom not too small.
Creation is your work.
The energy locked in the smallest particle is your power.
Your presence sustains it all, turning the wheels of change.
Of life and death, birth and renewal.
This is your world,
and somehow all the joy and hope
and life and pain are yours.
And the impossible is true —
in all the turmoil of life,
in the constant movement of stars,
of old worlds dying and new worlds exploding into life,
you have time for people.

Lord, when things are tense and I'm stretched to the limit today,
by people, and noise,
or by the ache of loneliness in a quiet room,
let me feel you near.
Help me to see that the problems I face
are faced by others too.
It may hurt my ego to know I'm not unique
that others face the same,
but it's a comfort too.
It's not that I'm singled out for problems beyond the next person.
It's just that I'm living in a world where these things happen.
And although I don't always get an answer when I ask "Why?"
somehow I get the strength to cope.
And that's you, Lord,
the God of the impossible, coming to me where I am.
Sometimes cooling it,
sometimes letting things run on,
but always offering your help if only I'll stop and take it.

Lord, teach me to keep my problems in perspective.
And help me to reach out, away from myself,
to others in need.
To share with them the experience I have
of the impossible made possible in you.

Philippians 4:10-13

THERE is a great danger in over-simplifying the Christian faith; in glossing over the hard bits. My mind picked up a phrase recently, I don't remember where, which said baldly, "Whom God calls, He enables." In simple English, rather than standard Christian jargon, it simply says that when God asks you to do something, He gives you the strength to do it. Paul put it more memorably to Christians at Philippi: "I have strength for anything through Him who gives me power" (Phil. 4:13). To both statements I would say, "Yes . . . but . . .", and the "but" would say that it isn't quite as simple as it sounds, and that Paul wouldn't want it taken in isolation from all the other experiences he had had — including the times of frustration and stress.

Think of Moses, representing God's will to Pharaoh. It wasn't easy. Moses conquered his early reluctance to act as God's mouth-piece, but then met doubts from his own people, the Hebrews, and found Pharaoh stubborn and uncooperative. Moses wasn't an automaton, he was human, a man with hopes and fears and anxieties. And beneath the simplicity of the story of Moses, facing the Egyptian King, coming back repeatedly to the same problem, the same theme, the imagination pictures the frustration he felt. Sheer anger must surely have erupted from time to time; and dejection and exasperation when Pharaoh says "No" once more; and a growing reluctance to try again. When one thinks of political negotiations today, extending over weeks and months, one wonders at the tensions hidden by the smooth communiques — "there was a full and frank exchange of views".

Yes, of course God helps us when He asks us to do something, Paul proved it, I've proved it, but it isn't in a fairy god-mother, wand-waving sort of way. He doesn't automatically put everything right or smooth out the road. His gift of "strength for anything" may as often be patience to bear, as a nice simple solution to apply. In fact, in my experience, it's more often the former than the latter. But that is no counsel of despair; it is a Christian realism that keeps us firmly in the world, to live, to work, to testify, that God is real, and that the faith is relevant. That sort of honest realisation gives me more hope, more to hold on to, than any statement of over-simplified evangelism. It is that sort of realism we need today.

And that is the sort of strength to expect from the Lord, not for the false security of ease —

> "Not for ever in green pastures
> Do we ask our way to be:
> But by steep and rugged pathways. . . ."

Lord, there are times when faith comes easy.
Times when things go right.
It all feels great,
and I'm tempted to believe
that it ought to be like that.
Always.

But then problems sneak up quietly,
or hit me hard over the head
and I want to creep away to hide in a corner.
To suck my thumb.
And I look at you resentfully.

Why does it happen to me, Lord?
Why are you picking on me?

And then there are the demands you make, Lord.
Your challenge.
The things you expect me to do.
To live your way.
To show your love in my life.
How can I cope with this on top of everything else?
I expect you to do something, to smooth the path again,
to make everything fairy-tale easy.
To drive away the wicked witch and all the monsters.
Where's the magic wand, Lord, and the happy ending?

And then the small voice.
The words in my mind, soft but insistent.
"My grace is sufficient for you."
But Lord, the problem's still here,
it hasn't gone away.
I have a busy schedule . . .
It's not possible in my circumstances . . .

"My grace is sufficient. . . ."

Yes, Lord.
It's not easy but I'll try.
I know you are with me.
I know that your hand will guide me,
even though I can't see the road.
Even though it's stony, and it all seems too much.
Help me to reach out for your strength.
It's there for me to take.
Not a magic wand — I'm not a child any more.
And I know the world isn't like that.
And I know that you know.
Because it's your world and you walk in it.
Thank you, Lord.

Luke 24:13-16

HE was a prophet "mighty in deed and word", said the disciples to the stranger on the Emmaus road (Luke 24:20). Perhaps it was the shock of radical change which prevented them from recognising Jesus, or the fact that they were still using the past tense about Him ... *"was a prophet"*. Their failure to recognise their Lord is something we need to think about and relate to our own circumstances. Their experience of Jesus was in the past, and they thought they were alone. The cross had taken Him from them, and their minds had not made sense of the changed situation, or adjusted to it. In this change Jesus was somehow out of context; they couldn't fit Him into the picture. In a way it worries me that they didn't recognise Him, but that's what the Gospel says, and we have to accept it whether we understand or not.

But do we always recognise Him, beside us? Hard work, routine, tiredness, ill health, can so grind us down that we carry on mechanically, never lifting our eyes — or minds — from the dust of the road, unaware of the glory and strength of His presence with us. Life gets thin and weak, the meaning drains out, leaving us with the dry, washed-out dregs. Yet He is still there, as the "stranger", walking with us, talking to us, listening when we speak. As the two disciples spoke of the cross, He took hold of their bewilderment and sorrow, and "beginning with Moses and the prophets" helped them to make sense of it. Sharing their problem with Him brought them towards a solution.

There is a more profound truth in it too — Christ isn't there beside us simply to help us find solutions — He is often in the problem itself. The problem for the two disciples was how to make sense of the cross, how to accept it. Jesus helped them to do that, but He also showed them that the cross itself was the creative act of God, and that He was *in* the problem, as well as in the solution.

Looking back at some of the difficulties I have faced over the past years, I begin to see God's hand in them — pushing the problem at me to stimulate and challenge me to rethink and to reshape my relationships. There are times when a problem looks as though it was sent to break us, but it ends by building us up — Christ in the problem itself, and Christ with us, helping us towards honest thinking; supporting and guiding us to the point where He wants us. "Tried in the fire" — there was a time when I thought of that as an Old Testament attitude which tried to rationalise piously (can you rationalise piously?) the things that were wrong in the world. Now, perhaps, I see a little less dimly, and can, I hope, recognise the presence of the Lord a little more clearly in the problems as I walk through the dust of the road. Does it help you to look for the presence of Christ IN your problems? Try it; one day you may be able to thank Him for them, although that's harder!

They felt alone, Lord,
as they walked towards Emmaus.
The stony ground, the dust,
the road, rutted and rough, meant nothing.
Neither did the stranger, coming from nowhere,
breaking in on their grief.
There was nothing left but memories
and they were still harsh and painful.
Time had had no chance to smooth the rough edges.
Their emotions were raw and bleeding.

Lord, I don't want to dramatise,
but I know how they felt.
I've stood in the wreckage of my plans,
seeing nothing but disappointment.
Shrugging my shoulders,
trying to pretend I didn't care.
Turned off.
Then you appeared. Unexpected.
And the world was good again.
Not like Cinderella and the fairy godmother,
rags to riches, pumpkin to coach, mice into horses.
(I've always felt sorry for the mice, Lord,
everyone forgets about them.)
Not like that.
The pain didn't suddenly disappear.
Outwardly there was little change,
but the air smelled fresher, the knots relaxed.
I began to function again,
to respond to other people,
and to see you.

Lord, it's good to know you are with me,
in all the strains life brings.
In the disappointments and difficulties
let me feel your presence.
And, Lord, help me to share this with others.
Make my presence with them your presence.
May your Spirit in me encourage and strengthen.
And as I recognise Jesus walking beside me,
may others see something of him in me.

Lord, thank you,
because you are always here.

Acts 14:19-22

ONE of my most treasured experiences is that of speaking in the main Moscow Baptist Church to the Sunday congregation. It was the third service of the day — Sunday evening — and the church was packed with eight hundred people, eager to listen to what I had to say. My wife and I returned to the church the following Tuesday evening for a baptismal service; 12 women, and 3 men, young and old, confessing their faith in Christ through believers' baptism. After three sermons, several hymns, anthems and prayers, a request came from the congregation, asking if the brother from England could speak again. I reminded them of Philippians 4:13: "I can do all things through Christ, who strengthens me." This text has meant much to me. It does not say "I can do all things easily," or without effort or difficulty, but it promises His strength in our work and witness for Him. The comment brought a response from those listening, living as they must under some stress. And yet, difficult or not, there was great joy and loving concern within the fellowship.

In Acts 14 there is a situation of stress. After preaching in Lystra Paul had been stoned and left for dead. He recovered, went on, but later returned to Lystra, deliberately going out of his way to do so. Why? To "put fresh heart into the disciples, encouraging them to persevere in the faith". Neither weariness nor danger could prevent Paul from doing what he felt was right. He accepted danger and stress because the believers needed him, knowing in his heart that his Lord would give him the necessary strength. Perhaps it is worth meditating, for a few minutes, on these situations. They will say different things to each of us in relation to our own lives and work, and the stresses we live under. It says something to me, in my situation; I hope it does to you.

Lord, whatever I may say, I have it easy.
You know I've got problems —
you should, I spend most of my prayer time
telling you about them;
and often, forgive me,
telling you exactly how I want them solved.
But when I look around with eyes and mind open
and see what others have to face
then I know — I have it easy.

There are so many people living in places
where following you
really does mean abandoning friends and family,
and where danger is real.
Lord, I don't know how I'd live in that situation.
Whether I'd have the guts to go on,
or whether I'd mingle with the crowd.
It's easy to say "I'd stand up for you"
but I remember Peter.

I don't know, Lord, I don't know.
What I do know
is that there is strength and courage
in seeing what they do in your power.
And from knowing that in Christ they can do all things.
It's not easy.
It takes sweat and tears
but it can be done.
And if they can, I can.
Because you are standing with me too.
Not only in Moscow
but in London, Calcutta, Hong Kong.

Wherever I am.
Your promise is for me.
It has to be, it's the only way,
because I can't do it on my own.

Then there was Paul,
not only enduring, but going back.
Returning to danger,
putting fresh heart into the rest.
That's something else, Lord,
but maybe I can do that too,
where I am, now.

There are folk around me
with bigger problems than mine.
Frightened, anxious and lonely,
wanting a little bit of human contact.

Needing a little courage to face problems and hang on to life.
I can encourage them
just by being with them, just by listening.
Just by taking off a bit of their load,
like you take mine.
Is that what you want me to do?
I can't do it on my own — but thank you, Lord,
I don't have to.

Korean Village

John 10:1-10

THE two acre site was muddy, with a squalid pool of green water in the centre. A thousand people were living there, refugees from the floods and famine which have created such havoc in Bangladesh. Conditions were primitive, people crowded into long shelters, each family trying to define a little area it could cling to and identify. I toured the refugee camp, one of several in Dacca, with the Dutch Salvation Army officer in charge. It was a grim picture: matchstick-limbed, potbellied children with kwashiorkor, covered in impetigo, sitting roundbacked and listless, eyes dull and still. Family groups: a man sitting with his wife and three children. He, nursing a sick and very weak baby, waiting for it to die. Folk too bewildered and beaten to do anything; some dying of disease, some dying from sheer despair.

In the West, Government departments wonder how much they should do to help, how much the taxpayer will stand, what political advantages their "Aid" may bring. I came across a quote the other day. Trevor Beeson, writing on a different subject, said: "Food for myself is a material question. Food for my neighbour is a spiritual one."

If I see my neighbour in need, *his* problem may be physical, but *my* reaction to his need is dependent on my spiritual growth and sensitivity. If I turn my back on my neighbour's hunger or illness to concentrate on a "spiritual" ministry can it be born of genuine concern? "I am come that men may have life ... in all its fullness" said Jesus. The point really is that the artificial separation of Christian life and witness into compartments limits our concept and experience of God's loving concern. I believe all life is "religious" — that its purpose is to enable us to grow nearer to God, to share in the fullness of life with Him; and to experience the redeeming touch of Christ's hand in every aspect of life. We should be content with nothing less than a full Christian ministry, embracing the total need of the total man.

Why, Lord?

It's the eyes I remember.
The child, potbellied and limp like a broken doll.
The dull eyes not moving, unfocussed, still.
The mother's eyes, dry from too many tears. No words.
Just looking, first at her baby, and then at me.
The man asking a quiet question in a foreign language.
He thought I didn't understand, but I did.
I just thought it easier not to.
And the others, all the same. All different.
"I am come that men may have life . . . in all its fullness."
Lord — I daren't even ask the question
but you can read it in my heart.

Why, Lord?
Why am I where I am? With my work and home,
and food for months sitting there in the freezer.
It's not fair. I don't understand.
And as I look up, I see you, Lord, on the cross.
And it's the eyes again. Your eyes full of agony and love.
I can hear you, Lord, I can hear.
"If you want a reason look into yourself!"
Whether it's the broken child, or broken God on the cross,
the cause is the same.
It's me Lord. It's my problem, and all mankind's.
Charity begins at home. Mine does. And ends there.
But I gave to Christian Aid . . . generously.
What more, Lord? Is it my life you want?
The problem is I like it the way it is,
and even my pain for others doesn't go very deep.
I want to change the world, Lord, and I can't even change my pew!
It has to start with me, my life style, my values, my judgements.
Lord, help me, because it's only when I change, that others may.
And it's only when others change that things change.
It's only then that eyes will shine,
not with tears, but with laughter.
Only when I change can I face those eyes.
The child's eyes, your eyes.
They are all the same.

Acts 20:35

"HAPPINESS lies more in giving than in receiving," says Paul, quoting an otherwise unrecorded saying of Jesus (Acts 20:35). In the context of material need I'm sure we all agree, but sometimes I believe we misapply it. It may be more *blessed* to give, but it may be more *helpful* to receive. The trouble is, it's harder. I'm not referring to material things of course, I'll accept Paul's word there! I'm thinking of attitudes, and of a dangerous trap into which so many Christians fall. All our motivation seems to be towards giving. Whether it's the Good News, or advice, or skills, we put ourselves in the role of donor, and the more we develop the desire to give the less we are able to receive.

It is so easy to teach, to tell; so difficult to learn, to listen. I remember very early days in India when I was talking to a group of leprosy patients at a time when I was just beginning to gain some confidence. Correction — not "talking" — "laying down the law" would be more accurate. The group listened patiently (do you realise how longsuffering people often have to be with us?). Then there was a stirring and an old man, a Muslim, blind, disabled, weak, quietly said, "But, sir, that would not be just." Thank God I listened to him. The situation which seemed so simple, so obvious, was a bit more complex than my arrogance and inexperience could see. I listened, I think I learned something, and I was saved from making a mistake. There were other occasions when I didn't listen and I made mistakes, because it takes a special grace to receive, and more to receive graciously, and we are not always ready to do it.

Part of the problem is that giving, whether we admit it or not, is a nice, satisfying ego-trip. We like it. It feels good. But ego doesn't have much of a place in the Christian life. There are those difficult bits in the New Testament about sacrifice, and crosses, and putting other people before self, and however much we ignore them they won't go away. It is an important, essential part of Christian maturity to be able to pause and listen, even if sometimes we don't like what we hear. It is not just for our own sakes but to help others to grow, for them to find a chance to share, to "minister" to us. Try going to a "junior" colleague and asking how he or she would do something, and see how he expands, grows, and feels better. Remember the gracious way Jesus accepted Mary washing His feet? And do you recall the roughness of Peter's first reaction when Jesus started to wash his feet? It's a humbling contrast.

Am I always the teacher, the giver, in my set-up; am I always right? Or have I learned a little about receiving, and listening? Just as important — have you? When we move away from the infallibility of the giver, the one who knows, and learn to acknowledge that others have things to give to us, it can take some of the tensions out of life. It's hard being up on a pedestal, it's so easy to fall off; and it's more painful falling off than staying on the ground with the rest of us.

It's a complicated business, Lord,
when you think about it.
You have given me so much
and I want to give to others in my turn.
Not to set myself up in your place,
but to show you that I care.
And people do need help.
But, Lord, help me to step back a minute
and look at what I'm doing,
like a painter stepping back to see the whole picture.

It's so easy to see myself as a giver.
And it feels good.
I'll admit I sometimes resent the demands
on my time, and energy and money.
Sometimes going the second mile is tiring
and I'd rather be home watching television.
But it still feels good, when it's done,
to know that I've helped.
To remember the thankyou I got
at the end of the hospital visit.
The appreciation "for services rendered"
to the old folk round the corner,
and for sharing the problems of that young married couple
having difficulties together.

And I'm not putting it down, Lord.
People need help, the sort of help I can give.
But help me, Lord, not to get so busy giving to others
that I can't receive from them.
Protect me from being so full of my own importance
that I can't admit my need of others.
So caught up in the pride of self-sufficiency
that I can't admit I need help.
And when someone tries to do something for me
show me how to accept it graciously.
To acknowledge their right to give, to feel needed,
even when it's not really what I wanted.
Even when the giving is clumsy
and I'm a bit embarrassed by it,
Lord, let me take it in the right spirit.
Lovingly.
Because we need each other.

Romans 12:1-2

FESTO KIVENGERE, exiled Bishop of Kigezi, who left Uganda under threat of death, said "I was asked how I would react if I were handed a gun and President Amin were sitting opposite me. The only reply that I could give was that I would hand the gun to the President and say, 'I think this is your weapon. It is not mine. My weapon is love.'" I found it a moving statement. It is not simply a picture of a man advocating non-violence, or making a stand for a Christian brand of pacifism, but of someone refusing to allow violence and evil to dictate his own reaction, or to subtract anything from the dignity of his humanity. Here is a human being, recreated by God as God wants him, living by the values he has taken as his own, and not allowing himself to be pulled down to the level of violence by a violent man; refusing to become angry in response to anger. Maintaining his own integrity, his own personality.

It is the integrity of Christ, facing the world's evil at work through Pilate and Caiaphas, and going on to the cross because any other way would have brought Him to the level of His accusers. It is sacrificial, as St. Paul grasped ". . . Be not conformed . . ." or as the NEB puts it — "Adapt yourselves no longer to the pattern of this present world . . ." (Romans 12:2). It is not an easy way, but it is the fulfilment of personality through identification with Christ. This is the only way to be true to ourselves as recreated people in Christ. Christ frees us to be our true selves and not what others would make us. It is a gift I crave very much — to be able to choose not to react at the level of provocation; not to be awkward with someone because he is; not to respond in kind to a sarcastic remark; not to want to hurt when I am hurt. To love, whatever the circumstances. What a difference it would make to us all, and the communities we live in, to be in control of ourselves at that level — not to give a feeling of superiority, not to suggest that we are better than the rest, but as a measure of our identity with Christ and of the degree to which He has taken over in deed and word. Because it is not really that we control ourselves — although it is our volition and effort — but that Christ is doing it. "And yet not I, but Christ who lives within me. . . ."

Lord, how did you do it?
How did you manage to keep quiet,
in the face of taunts and violence?
How were you able to respond with love
when you saw the hate and evil in their faces?
It must have been hard,
especially knowing you were innocent.
I find it hard too.
Not just the experience but the response.
I can usually find the sarcastic answer.
And when someone gets angry with me,
I can usually shout as loud as he can.
I can't remember it coming to blows,
not since I was in the school playground,
but my muscles still tighten
and I can feel the rage welling up.
And I look at you again.
I look through my anger, and the resentment
which clouds my sight and reduces my vision.
I see you still and gentle.
Gentle. Not weak.
Filled with the courage to stand firm.
Not to be provoked.
Not to give way to the mindless anger and violence around you.
Filled with love
because you see the frightened man behind the bluster.

Lord, give me that insight, that sensitivity.
Let me see the insecurity behind his shouting,
so that I can try to reassure.
Let me see the hurt behind the curse
so that I can heal.
Let me hear the cry for help
just beneath the surface of his stubborn pride,
and respond with understanding.
Lord, I can't do it, not on my own.
The world is strong.
I can't fight my instincts. I must keep my pride.
And then I look at you again, and I know I'm not alone.
I offer myself to you, a living sacrifice.
I'm beginning to see what that means.
I still find it hard, Lord,
but, share it with me.
Share it. Please.

Galatians 5:22-25

"THE diffrense from a person and an angel is easy. Most of an angel is in the inside and most of a person is on the outside." So says six-year-old Anna in *Mister God, This is Anna*, written by Fynn and published in Collins paperbacks. It is a string of pearls, sensitive insights into the nature of God in conversations between Anna and her friend Fynn. I had been reading two books on the flight to Bombay — this one, and *Season on the Plain* by Franklin Russell, a beautifully written, vivid description of life and death among the animals of the East African plain. All the prodigality of nature was there, the waste of myriad lives, the apparently mindless sacrifice of individuals to group welfare. "Anna" brought me back from the suffering and pain of so much of nature to an assertion of God's loving concern for the individual. To be honest the two views are difficult to reconcile. One is observable, and the other experiential, yet equally valid and whatever the waste and suffering, God cares.

Anna goes on to Fynn, "You love me because you are people. I love Mister God truly, but he don't love me. . . . No, he don't love me, not like you do, it's different, it's millions of times bigger . . . Mister God is different. . . . People can only love outside and can only kiss outside, but Mister God can love you right inside and kiss you right inside . . . Mister God ain't like us; we are a little bit like Mister God but not much yet."

"Fynn thought 'As far as Anna was concerned, being good, generous, kind, praying, were merely a spin off. Religion was all about *being* like Mister God, and it was here that things could get a little tough. The instructions weren't to be good and kind and loving and therefore you would be more like Mister God. No! The whole point of being alive was to *be* like Mister God and then you couldn't help but be good and kind and loving, could you?' "

And so it goes on. It's a great book, with a lot to say to many of us. As I travel I see folk working so hard to do a good job, some successfully, others with difficulty, and sometimes the problem is that they are starting at the wrong end. Trying to legislate rather than to *be*. Sure, we need rules and basic standards, but we show the faith, and Christ, not in simply living the rules but in "being like Mister God". We can show that love outside only when Mister God is right inside. It takes longer, it's tougher and there are no short cuts — but it works. And Anna puts in a little sting at the end, "and if you get like Mister God, you don't know you are, do you?" — But others do!

Lord, it's easy setting up rules.
Easy to persuade myself
that if only I could live by them you'd be pleased.
And I'd be happy.
The trouble is I can't even live by my own rules.
It doesn't work out.
It's not that my standards are too high, too stringent.
It's just that I don't have the strength, the consistency.
Not on my own.
And no matter how hard I try,
the love, joy, peace
and all the rest of it
is pretty thin on the ground.

Lord, help me to realise I'm starting at the wrong end.
When I look at you, Lord
I can't quite tell if you are crying at my misery
or laughing at my foolishness.
Because there you are offering me the answer.
Free.
Yourself.
All I have to do is to open up my life
and let you in.
It's not all that easy, Lord,
because when I do it I've got to let everything else go.
But it's good, Lord.
Because when you take over my world changes.
The rules don't matter anymore.
And the life I live is your life.

You living in me.
Working in me.
Changing me.
Watering the seeds of love, joy, peace,
which you brought in and planted.
They grow slowly, in fits and starts.
Sometimes the dark turns their leaves yellow and limp.
But they do grow.
Surely.
Because you are there, working.
Not from the outside, but from within.

Gradually building me
in your own image.

Colossians 1:15-20

"JESUS is Lord. It is He by whom all things exist. It was He who spiralled the DNA Helix, who choreographed the genetic quadrille in cell division, who scored the hormonal symphony, and who heals the wounds which we bind up ... and by looking to this Lord, the Doctor of Galilee, this Sustainer of every galaxy, we can day by day calibrate our behaviour."

The quote is from a Christian doctor in this country, whose name I don't know. It isn't the usual language of devotion but to me it suggests something fundamental — that Jesus is Lord of TODAY.

Sometimes we Christians live in the past, in the West anyway. Our traditions, our well-loved hymns, the thought patterns and language of worship, often suggest a clinging to the old and comfortable — for security, and as a defence against the anxieties of living in an unstable and unpredictable world. At other times we see Jesus as Lord of the future. We look ahead to the "summing up of all things" and the time when He will "make all things new". I'm not knocking the past — it's a source of inspiration to me to feel part of a great cosmic movement of worship, prayer and service going back two thousand years to Jesus. Yes, and beyond that too, and to look back in wonder at the unfolding experience of the love of Christ in my own life. Neither am I knocking the future — it's not "pie in the sky", but an assurance which gives purpose and meaning to today.

But what of NOW? That's what we have to live in, and if faith doesn't make sense of NOW, it makes sense of nothing. It's no good thinking of the past or future Christ if we are not meeting Him today, and experiencing His presence in the opportunities and frustrations of our world. Is there sometimes a feeling of being distant from Him? But He is close by — in your neighbour, looking at you through the sick eyes of a patient, asking for understanding as you listen at your end of a telephone — the Lord of today. He is the NOW of my world and yours, the now of the universe because, personal Lord though He is, it is also true that "all things are held together in him" (Col. 1:17) — the primal statement of faith and the root of reassurance. He comes, not as a visitor to our world but as the Lord and Sustainer of it, the focus and fulcrum of it all — and yet available to each one of us.

Lord, my mind is so small.
And it makes you small.
I reduce you to a size I can live with.
I can't encompass all that you are.
I can't comprehend the vastness, the power,
that are yours.

Lord of all things,
Lord of all time. And of eternity.
Lord of creation.
Your hand bringing together the atoms, energy.
Your hand bringing order out of chaos.
Light out of darkness.
Breathing life into the world
and setting laws for its sustaining.

Lord of history.
Gathering up the past.
Using nations and people
to reveal yourself through their lives,
showing your love and concern
that we might know the truth which can set us free.

Lord of the future.
There are so many uncertainties, Lord.
So many things to worry about.
Men don't seem to get much better
in the way they run things.
But I believe that one day
— although I don't waste my time trying to work out when —
one day
I shall see your power and glory,
when all things are made new.

So the past and the future are safe, Lord.
That's not the problem.
My problem is NOW.
I can live in the past.
I can crawl into it like a womb,
warm and safe from the harsh winds of reality.
I can bury my head in the future,
ignoring the uncertainty of today in dreams and visions.

The problem is NOW.
Trying to make sense of what is happening today.
Trying to cope with today's crisis.
The latest famine.
Running out of bread for breakfast this morning.
Power politics.

Finding my train ten minutes late, and crowded.
Large and small. Significant or not.
It all adds to the strain, Lord.
And I need you NOW.

Not as a refuge.
Not as a dream.
As a companion.
As someone to walk with me on the road.

Autumn Poplars, Korea

THE LEPROSY MISSION INTERNATIONAL

50 Portland Place, London W1N 3DG

Australia:	7 Ellingworth Parade, Box Hill 3128, Vic.
Belgium:	rue de Stalle 62, 1180 Brussels
Canada:	40 Wynford Drive, Suite 216, Don Mills, Ontario M3C 1J5
Denmark:	Anemonevej 37, 2970 Hørsholm
England and Wales:	50 Portland Place, London W1N 3DG
Europe:	chemin de Rêchoz, 1027 Lonay/VD, Switzerland
Finland:	Harjutie 24A 1, SF-02730, Espoo 73
France:	37 rue Davioud, 75016 Paris
Ireland (Northern Area):	44 Ulsterville Avenue, Belfast BT9 7AQ
Ireland (Southern Area):	20 Lincoln Place, Dublin 2
Italy:	Via Pasteur 60, 18012 Bordighera (IM)
Netherlands:	Kooikersdreef, 626 7328 BS Apeldoorn
New Zealand:	43-45 Mount Eden Road, Auckland 3
Norway:	Viges veg 20, N-3700 Skien
Scotland:	26 Bothwell Street, Glasgow G2 6NU
South-East Asia:	14 Oakdale Road, Hillsborough, Auckland, New Zealand
Southern Africa:	PO Box 89527 Lyndhurst, 2106 Johannesburg
Southern Asia:	4th Floor, Sheetla House, 73-74 Nehru Place, New Delhi 110019, India
Spain:	Calle Bravo Murillo 85, Madrid 3
Sweden:	Nygatan 58, S 702 11 Orebro
Switzerland (French):	chemin de Rêchoz, 1027 Lonay/VD
Switzerland (German):	4622 Egerkingen, Postfach 22
W. Germany:	Hellerweg 51, 73 Esslingen/N
Zambia:	Box 30636, Lusaka
Zimbabwe:	24 Divine Road, Milton Park, PO Belvedere, Salisbury